The Passion for Life

The Passion for Life

A Messianic Lifestyle

by
JÜRGEN MOLTMANN

*Translated
with an
Introduction
by*
M. DOUGLAS MEEKS

FORTRESS PRESS   *Philadelphia*

This book is a freely adapted translation by M. Douglas Meeks of texts which appeared in slightly different form in the author's *Neuer Lebensstil. Schritte zur Gemeinde,* copyright ©1977 by Chr. Kaiser Verlag in Munich, Germany.

Biblical quotations from the Revised Standard Version of the Bible, copyright 1946, 1952, © 1971, 1973 by the Division of Christian Education of the National Council of the Churches of Christ in the U.S.A., are used by permission.
Biblical quotations from *The New English Bible,* © The Delegates of the Oxford University Press and The Syndics of the Cambridge University Press, 1961, 1970, are reprinted by permission.

Published in Great Britain under the title *The Open Church* by SCM Press Ltd., 1978.

Library of Congress Cataloging in Publication Data

Moltmann, Jürgen.
  The passion for life.

  A freely adapted translation of Neuer Lebensstil: Schritte zur Gemeinde.
  1. Church—Addresses, essays, lectures.
  2. Christian life—1960   —Addressess, essays, lectures. I. Meeks, M. Douglas. II. Title.
  BV603.M43 1977   260   77-78636
  ISBN 0-8006-0508-X

6453H77   Printed in the United States of America   1-508

For the
Moravian Theological Seminary
as a token of thanks for the bestowal of
the degree of Doctor of Divinity
and as a sign of friendship with
The Herrnhuter Brüdergemeinde

Contents

Preface

The chapters of this book arose out of the life of the congregation and are meant to serve the formation of a lively congregation. They come out of praxis and speak directly to
praxis. In them I would like to speak to members of the congregation not as a pastor or a theology professor but as a
member of the congregation. Thus I have refrained from
scholarly reflections and have provided only a few notes at the
back of the book. For those readers who might be interested,
some of the concepts in this book are developed more exten-
sively in my book *The Church in the Power of the Spirit: A
Contribution to Messianic Ecclesiology.*

What cannot be said simply does not need to be written at
all. Simplicity is the highest challenge to Christian theology.
Theology stands under the demand to speak simply because,
as Christian theology, it stands or falls with the church. But
the church stands or falls with the gathered congregation, the
mature community, the open friendship of Jesus. This is why
the scientifically trained theologian is, above all else, a
member of this gathered congregation. And every member of
this congregation who believes and thinks is a theologian. In
the history of the church of Christ there have been good times
in which theology and congregation lived in intimate
mutuality and were molded together in unit in the face of op-
position and trial. It is my expectation that theology will increasingly enter into the practice and experience of the people
and that the congregation will more and more come to express
its pains and joys in theology.

Some of the chapters of this book were first given as lectures
during a memorable trip through the United States in

September and October 1976. In naming these stations on the way I also greet the friends who are in each place: The Holy Cross Abbey, Canon City, Colo.; The Immaculate Heart Community, Montecito, Calif.; Pacific School of Religion, Berkeley, Calif.; Stanford University, Calif.; St. Mark's Cathedral, Seattle, Oreg.; Moravian Theological Seminary, Bethlehem, Pa.; The American Baptist Convention, Providence, R.I.; Andover Newton Theological School, Newton Centre, Mass.; Princeton Theological Seminary, Princeton, N.J.; Union Theological Seminary, New York; Lutheran Theological School, Gettysburg, Pa.; Duke University, Durham, N.C.; University of North Carolina, Chapel Hill, N.C.; Lutheran Theological Southern Seminary, Columbia, S.C.; Eden Theological Seminary, St. Louis, Mo.

I am deeply grateful to my friend Douglas Meeks for the work of the translation, for encouragement in conversations, and for joy in friendship.

Tübingen   JÜRGEN MOLTMANN

ACKNOWLEDGMENTS

I am grateful for the translation work of Martha Corcoran on chapter 4, "Open Friendship," and of Ralph Klein and Erwin Lueker on chapter 1, "The Passion for Life."

Chapter 1, "The Passion for Life," originally appeared in *Currents in Theology and Mission* 4 (February, 1977), and chapter 6, "The Ecumenical Church under the Cross," originally appeared in *Theology Digest* 24 (Winter, 1976).

M. Douglas Meeks

Introduction

M. DOUGLAS MEEKS

It is indeed eventful when a major German systematic theologian attempts to do theology from the perspective of a layperson in the congregation. The split between academic theology and the experience of ordinary Christians may not be once and for all overcome in this book, but Jürgen Moltmann has set out here with the clear recognition of the futility of a Christian theology which is not devoted to the life of the congregation.

Modern theology has often given lip service to Christian theology's dependence on the church. The so-called father of modern Protestant theology, Friedrich Schleiermacher, was aware of this when he began his great dogmatic work with this thesis: "Since dogmatics is a theological discipline, and thus pertains solely to the Christian church, we can only explain what it is when we have become clear as to the conception of the Christian church."* Theologians down through Barth and Tillich have echoed this assumption. But this insight can remain abstract if theology is not also aware from the beginning that the life and future of the church is wrapped up with the gathered congregation. Unfortunately modern theology has been unwilling to accept this second truth as a presupposition of its work.

And understandably so! The formation of the Christian congregation has become increasingly difficult in the industrial-technocratic world in which Freud wondered whether it might not be impossible after all to form any kind of community. Thus theology has preferred to deal, on the one hand, with the question of how to know the truth of Christianity from its

13

tradition and, on the other hand, with the question of how to relate this truth to the modern world. This has resulted in the well-known gap between "theologies of the church" and "theologies of the world."

In recent times various theologies of the Christian mission to the contemporary world have tried to bridge this gap. But these theologies also retain a certain speculative cast when they are not related to an actually existing bearer of the Christian mission in the world. If theology develops the finest theory possible without attending to the question of who is going to practice this theory, it remains suspended in the realm of possibilities. Thus, as theory of the Christian mission, theology must be passionately devoted to the life of the congregation. Whatever else its task might be, theology has constantly to serve the creation of the congregation as a viable historical reality. Otherwise the work of theology has the tinge of vanity.

This book addresses itself to the question of how the Christian congregation can be formed at all. What we in Europe and North America glibly call "congregations" often have no resemblance to what the Reformation originally envisioned as the congregated people of God. During the last 450 years the Protestant churches have nearly destroyed one of the principal realities at which the Reformation was aiming, namely, the congregation. There is nothing in principle wrong with structures, organization, authority, and offices in the church. They are all necessary. What is wrong is the way in which all of these have come to be understood and practiced in an over-clericized, authoritarian, and statically structured church. The problem with such a church is that the life of the congregation gets squeezed out. When the vitality of the congregation atrophies and disappears the church becomes nothing but an empty shell and there is nothing to embody and bear the liberating mission of God in this world.

Some readers of this book may have the impression that the formation of the congregation is not the main problem in most of our denominations. It may seem that the problems Moltmann is dealing with are peculiarly German problems. After all, in the English-speaking world by and large we do not have established state churches. Moreover the "free church" and congregational traditions have had a certain influence in our midst. But a sober scrutiny of our churches will reveal that these very traditions, of which we are justly proud, have also been effectively repressed. There is nothing more urgent for the future of Christianity in the English-speaking world than to recover our "free church" and congregational traditions, so that what the Reformation meant by "congregation" can appear in our time. Even though our churches are not *Volkskirchen* (national or cultural churches) in the strict sense, they nevertheless manifest many of the charteristics of the *Volkskirche*. Our churches have become bureaucratic, vertical in organization, overly clerical in identity, planned and directed "from above." They often militate against all those conditions necessary for the congregation to "come of age."

The maturation of the congregation is still the unfinished work of the Reformation; the mature congregation is the still open future of the Reformation. Most of our churches, in spite of their tremendously sophisticated skills in pastoral care and counseling, organizational development, sensitivity training, conflict management, and motivation workshops initiated and implemented from the top down, have simply been incapable of forming the mature congregation. Is it not a devastating irony that the more competent the "leadership" becomes in caring *for* the people, the less involved the people become and the less responsibility they feel for the church? Has our craze for practice-oriented skills and for "do-it-yourself" sociologies and psychologies of unburdening seduced the churches to become centers of private, individual compensation for the impersonal life of our everyday world?

How can the new identity of the congregation be found? The answer to this question is wrapped up in the question of how the people can be empowered to create through the Holy Spirit their own congregation for which they are truly responsible. If the Reformation churches are going to claim their open future, it will mean rediscovering many of those dimensions of the tradition about which most Protestant denominations have been most wary in recent times. Reformation congregations with a genuine future will have to become passionate, evangelical, diakonal, missional, ecumenical, charismatic, and esthetic.

Moltmann makes a persuasive case here that the most crucial thing the congregation has to regain today is passion. The words "passion" and "suffering" will be found in this book and may be somewhat puzzling to the reader because in their ordinary use they have lost much of their theological content. It may be said that one objective of Moltmann's recent theology is to rehabilitate the word "passion" for use in theology as well as everyday life in the church. This is necessary because the congregation lives out of the "passion" of Christ (which refers both to the *Leiden* or suffering of Jesus and to the *Leidenschaft* or passionate devotion of his life to God's reign of righteousness). The passion of God in Christ creates the church through the Holy Spirit.

Most of our ordinary usages of "suffer" are negative in connotation. "To suffer" usually connotes a passive subjection to pain or a passive endurance of something deleterious to our existence. In Middle English, however, the word "suffer" still retained the biblical sense of passion. It did not mean passivity. It implied an active as well as receptive power, and thus it was better able to convey the deepest of Christian truths: "the power of God" is "the word of the cross" (1 Cor. 1:18). "Passion" and "suffering" mean not simply to be acted upon but also to be affected, changed, transformed, and matured by the lives of others. To be open, accessible, vulnerable is not the sign of passive impotence but the precondition of active historical life. Suffering also means the power to go outside of oneself and affect the other. And thus it is the condition of love. One who is not empowered with suffering is not able to love, and vice versa. For Christian faith, suffering love is finally the greatest power thinkable or believable. "God is suffering love" (1 John 4:8), and suffering love is the greatest gift of the Holy Spirit to us. It is the power of the Holy Spirit which is promised to the congregation.

The increasing coldness of human life, the increasing inability to feel with others and thus to form communal relationships, is the most ominous threat to the human future in Western society. For without the formation of communities there can be no solutions to the dehumanization which is taking place in the political, economic, cultural, and natural dimensions of life. The power of passion is a gift which the Christian congregation can give to social existence. But the Christian church has no chance to mediate this power to society unless diakonia, mission, and ecumenism begin in and with the congregation itself. Only then can the congregation learn to be not only a church *for* others but more profoundly a church *with* others.

But the power of passion is in turn a gift of God in Jesus Christ through the Holy Spirit. This means that the congregation must be evangelical. The proclamation of the gospel's freedom to the poor means that the congregation will have a missionary identity. It finds its identity in its Author and Lord, Jesus Christ, who commissions it to give itself to the world. Evangelization and liberation, proclamation and mission are two sides of the same coin.

The congregation comes into existence in the first place through the power of the Spirit. Every Christian congregation must be formed charismatically by discovering the special gifts and talents which have been given by the Spirit to each person. All commissions, assignments, and functions belong first to the congregation as a whole. Hence all power rises "from the bottom up." Every member is called to and fully accountable for the whole life and mission of the congregation. Leaders and people are accountable to each other on the basis of everyone's accountability to the lordship and authority of Jesus Christ.

Moltmann suggests that a starting point for this task of forming the congregation lies in the domain of what is known in the Catholic church as ascetical theology. The question is how to give birth to a new messianic lifestyle in the congregation. For this an esthetic theology must be developed, and the theology of play expanded into a theory of messianic festivity. The congregation will view every member as an artist whose material is his or her own life, a life that is to be shaped according to the rich possibilities of the friendship that is created through the shape of Jesus' own life.

The congregation can and must become passionate, evangelical, diakonal, missional, ecumenical, charismatic, and esthetic. An exciting future lies ahead of us as we rediscover all these things which we have forgotten, sometimes intentionally.

1
The Passion
for Life

Where Jesus is, there is life. There is abundant life, vigorous life, loved life, and eternal life. There is life-before-death. I find it deeply disturbing and unsettling whenever I think about how we have become accustomed to death: to the death of the soul, to death on the street, to death through violence— to death-before-life.

"The worst thing is that one gradually becomes used to it." That's the way a friend in New York summed up his reaction to the growing crime rate as we were discussing a recent incident. That caused me to think. I believe he was right. Evil or suffering is not so bad in itself, but it is bad when we become "used to it," when we accept it, when we withdraw and become indifferent to it.

Young people in the best years of their lives are unemployed for prolonged periods—one becomes used to it. Hopelessness causes them to become addicts, dependent on drugs—one becomes used to it. In order to be able to buy the stuff out of which their false dreams are fashioned they daily need money and so become muggers—one becomes used to it. People are waylaid in bright daylight on open streets, knocked down and robbed—one becomes used to it. No one is aroused. And so such evil spreads like a cancer in a sick body. The vicious cycle of poverty, unemployment, crime, and prison becomes larger. Why? Because people become indifferent to other people, because they become numb and accept such things with a shrug of the shoulders, because they do not want to see the misery of other persons. In this way they try to escape their own suffering—and end up denying their own suffering. This is only one example of how day after day we admit death into our life, because we shrink from the conflict and no longer have a passionate devotion to life. There are others.

Think of our society's attitude toward the starving people of the third world, the hardcore unemployed, the migrant workers, the prisoners, the handicapped, and the so-called unfit. People such as these are ruined not because of *their* inability but because of *our* indifference. By our failure to participate or share in their lives, we neglect our own life. We isolate ourselves, we insulate our lives, we imprison ourselves in our own "good fortune."

For a physician apathy is a symptom of illness. The apathetic patient appears exhausted. He no longer participates in what is going on about him. His perceptions decline and his feelings die away. He no longer reacts to visits and conversation addressed to him. Cold indifference has taken hold of him. To me such apathy seems to be a characteristic sign of the illness of our society and of many individuals in it. Interest in life is crippled. The "courage to be" is weakened. One withdraws into a cell, boxes oneself in, locks oneself up in order not to be exposed to suffering, and so passes life by. One really doesn't live anymore but grows stiff in a living body.

What causes us to be so apathetic? What reduces a life so much that one can often hardly call it life anymore?

Apathy originally meant freedom from suffering, and in antiquity it was regarded as the highest virture of both gods and human beings: God is good and does no evil. God is perfect and cannot suffer. God is eternal and cannot die. God is sufficient unto himself and does not need friends. Apathy, freedom from suffering, belonged to divine perfection. A person who wanted to be like the gods had to learn and practice apathy. He had to overcome his needs and drives. The fulfillment of wishes did not bring happiness. Only the person who stopped wishing became happy. Therefore, a person had to be free of passionate feeling. One had to live without anger, but also without love. Pain and joy could no longer touch one. Overcome the desire to be, conquer your desires, become apathetic and you will become free and godlike at the same time!

The values and the ideas of our society are not very far

removed from this—except that apathy is no longer a voluntary virtue but a peculiar constraint from which human beings
can escape only with difficulty. The conquering of need,
dependence, and suffering through activity, work, and accomplishment is taken for granted by us. What are we longing
for? We strive for a life without suffering, for joy without pain,
for community without conflict. This is what we call "good
fortune." With such good fortune the capable and successful
among us, the people of achievement, are rewarded—
apparently.

I say "apparently" because this is not really the case;
"reward" is manifestly the wrong word. The idolatry which is
implicit in all our work, achievement, and success demands
sacrifice, as does all idolatry. The sacrifice we bring to the
idols of our desire and of our society are great. In our personal
life the one-sided orientation toward accomplishment and success makes us melancholic and insensitive. We become incapable of love and incapable of sorrow. We no longer have
tears, and we smile only because we are expected to keep smil-
ing all the time. Starvation in the third world no longer affects
us: "Those lazy, shiftless people ought to get to work!" We sup-
press our own pangs and disappointments: "I find that I am
happy only when I am working." Trusting the promises of the
gods of work and accomplishment we can perhaps attain a life
without pain and without conflicts, but we pay bitterly for it.
We become apathetic, still alive but slowly and surely dying
inwardly.

The one-sided orientation toward accomplishment and success makes us unjust and inhuman in our dealings with others.
We exclude the sick, the handicapped, the unaccomplished,
and the unsuccessful from public life. Also politically we have
to pay dearly for the gods of work and success. We have an
"apartheid" society. It may not in every case give privileges to
the whites over against the blacks, as in South Africa, but it
does give privileges to the healthy and capable over the re-
tarded and the weak. Instead of an open and vulnerable society, we have a closed and unassailable society with apathetic
structures. The living, open, vulnerable life is poured into
steel and concrete. That is the modern death called apathy:

life without suffering [*Leiden*], life without passionate feeling [*Leidenschaft*].

Formerly people would occasionally complain, "There is no longer any love left among people." Today it appears as though love for life itself is disappearing. Many fear that the world will end in atomic death. Others expect ecological death. It seems to me that we will come to ruin long before that by means of our own apathy. "The worst thing is that a person becomes used to it." Just as we became accustomed to crime in our big cities, so we have become accustomed to the threat of death through nuclear weapons (even raising the ante in the nuclear arms race) and to the destruction of our environment (even building more nuclear energy plants). We will become accustomed to death before it comes. Why? Because when the passionate devotion to life is missing, the powers to resist are paralyzed. Therefore if we want to live today, we must consciously *will* life. We must learn to love life with such a passion that we no longer become accustomed to the powers of destruction. We must overcome our own apathy and be seized by the passion for life.

I do not dispute that others find the courage for life and the power for suffering elsewhere. But for me this courage and power come again and again when I hold before me the picture of Christ. His passion for life led him to suffering on the cross. It is in his passion and his suffering that the passion of God becomes clear to me, and it is from God's passion that I receive the power to resist death.

Yet you hear people saying: "God cannot suffer." "God can never die." "God has no needs." "God needs no friends." Even Christians say things like that—and thereby make of the living God a dead idol, an idol constructed from their own anxiety about life.

The God about whom people spoke from experience in the Old and New Testaments, however, is no cold, silent, heavenly power that sits self-sufficiently upon his throne and scatters gracious alms among his subjects. He displays a great passion for creation, for human beings, and for the future. God's nearness is experienced in the breath of his pathos. And his pathos is his love for freedom, his passionate interest in life against death. Therefore, according to the Old Testament, he established a marriage-like covenant with the people. And so he became vulnerable in his love. When Israel turned away from him and fell into the hands of idols he suffered because of his passion for Israel's freedom. So he accompanied Israel on the way of suffering into exile. So he was angry at the stupid sins of human beings. But his wrath was an expression of his wounded love, nothing else.

If we were to live in a covenant with this passionate God, we would not become apathetic. Our whole life would be shaped by sympathy, by compassion. We would suffer with God's suffering in the world, and rejoice with God's rejoicing over the world. We would do both at the same time and with the highest intensity because we would love, and with the love of God we would go outside ourselves.

I once regarded as childish and human—all too human— the Old Testament ideas of a God who fumed with rage, who was jealous, who burned with love and could be disillusioned. The abstract god of the philosophers, purified of all human images, seemed to me nearer to the truth. But the more I experienced how abstraction destroyed life, the more I understood the Old Testament passion of God, and the pain which tore his heart. I was deeply moved to hear Jews say that the real suffering in the persecution of Israel was the suffering of God. God suffers with Israel. He goes with his people into exile, into concentration camps, into the gas chamber, into death. Their faith in the God who suffered with them preserved Israel against desperate self-destruction and against self-surrender through accommodation. When we discover in the depths of our own suffering the suffering of God we cannot become apathetic. We remain opposed to suffering; we abide in hope. Our own simple and insignificant suffering takes on meaning in the greater passion of God for a free and redeemed world.

The center of the New Testament is the history of the passion of Christ. One does not understand this passion history if one sees in it only one more tragic incident in the long history of humanity's suffering. One understands the history of Christ's suffering only when one grasps the passionate devotion of Christ which led him into it and allowed him to bear it. And in the passion of Christ I see the passion of God himself and discover again the passion of my own heart. In the history of the passion of Christ I perceive the pain of God himself and discover the pain of my own life which I have suppressed or projected onto others.

What is there about this life of Jesus that makes it speak to us again and again? I believe it is not one or another of the miracle stories but the entire life of great and passionate devotion that takes hold of us. Which passionate devotion? Not the yearning of the soul for a life free of pain in heaven, but the love for the kingdom of God in this world. Jesus' life is inspired not just by the wish for a life *after* death, but by the will for life *before* death, yes, even *against* death. Where the sick are healed, lepers are accepted, and sins are not punished but forgiven, there *life* is present. Freed life, redeemed life, divine life is there, in this world, in our times, in the midst of us.

Where Jesus is, there is life. The basic characteristic of the life of Jesus is not the consolation of the beyond, not even the hope in the future, but his becoming human, becoming flesh, his healing of life, accepting of the oppressed, and making alive the frozen relationships between human beings. For that reason we find in the company of Jesus all the woe of humanity—the demon possessed, the incurably diseased, the lame, the blind, the dumb, the dead: "those who are in darkness."* One sees them with Jesus and sees how they find life. Out of the dark corners of society into which we have condemned them they come into the limelight because they noticed the light, the life that Jesus spreads around himself through his guiding passion, through his love. In Jesus' passion for life the passion of God himself comes into view. That passion yearns for life and hates death; it desires freedom and hates slavery; it is love and knows no apathy.

Why did Jesus suffer, and what does his passion mean for us today? We know of course that he was crucified. Does this mean that he too failed? Does life have no other meaning than to die? Should a person be cautious about loving others in order to make dying easier? I do not find that Jesus failed at all at the end of his life. I rather ask how great must the passionate devotion be which is ready for such suffering? How great must the love for life be which suffered such a death? He was not condemned and executed by mistake. Jesus walked the way to Jerusalem consciously and purposely. He entered the city whose people suppressed life and threatened death. He came to this city for the life and freedom of the oppressed. For that reason he took on violent death by torture and execution.

Did that have to be? One might ask the question out of a kind of sympathy. Yet the more a person thinks about Jesus' death, the more inescapable it seems to be. Yes, the passionate devotion to life works contagiously only when it is prepared for suffering. The passion for freedom from the rigor of death makes one alive only when it brings along sacrifice. Basically, wounds are healed only by wounds. Not by superior power, but by his self-sacrifice does Christ bring life into view for those who suffer. The idols of power and of success do not help a person. Only a suffering God can help. "He bore our sickness and assumed our pains. By his wounds we are healed." With these words of the prophet regarding the suffering servant of God, the passionate devotion [*Leidenschaft*] and the suffering [*Leiden*] of Christ are summed up in the New Testament.

There is still another picture for it, the picture of the grain of wheat: "Unless a grain of wheat falls into the earth and dies, it remains alone; but if it does, it bears much fruit" (John 12:24). Whatever the biological facts may be, two things are important: if the grain of wheat remains alone, if it does not fall into the earth, it is unfruitful and basically dead. But if it falls into the earth, it becomes alive, even if it then dies. It does not remain as it was, but brings forth fruit through its transformation. "Remaining alone" is a meaningless death because it is a hopeless death. But surrender to the earth is a meaningful death because it is a fruitful dying. Herein I find the secret of the passionate dying of Jesus, and the secret of passion in our own life.

Human life is alive to the extent that it is loved and affirmed. The more passionately we love life, the more intensively we experience the joy of life. The more passionately we love life, the more we also experience the pain of life and the deadliness of death. We experience joy and pain, we become alive and mortal at one and the same time, not simply in life, but in that interest in life we call love. That is the twofold passion of life. The secret of life is very simple and sounds strange at the same time: He who would keep his life will lose it and is already losing it. He who, however, risks his life and surrenders it, will gain it and is gaining it already. To keep one's life means to hold onto oneself; one hardly dares to live because of one's sheer dread of death, or to love because one fears disappointment. The person who wants to keep his or her life in this way is not living at all. He or she remains basically "alone," that is, dead.

To give up one's life means to go outside oneself, to love, to expose oneself, and to spend oneself. In this passionate renunciation one's whole life becomes alive because it makes other life alive. If we live our lives in love we gain life even though we lose it physically. Those of us who really love life can also die; but the death of a loving life is not a hopeless death. Death is hopeless—and therefore horrible—only where life has not been lived and loved. What oppresses us in the hour of death, therefore, is not the life that has been lived and loved, but rather the life that has not been lived and that has neglected its possibilities. Indeed, an unlived, wasted life cannot die. This inability to die, which is experienced on a large scale in hospitals, is the bitter price of apathy, of lovelessness. Only the passion of love makes a person alive right down to the very fingertips. At the same time it makes a person able and ready to die.

That which abides in the passion of life, in the midst of living and dying, is *love*, the mysterious center of life and death, the passionate yes to life and the passionate no to the negation of life. Apathy is a terrible temptation. Promising to spare us death, it in fact takes away our life. It spreads the rigor of corpses and concrete around itself. Love makes life a passion, a matter of passionate devotion and readiness to suffer. If we take our bearings from the passion of God and the passion history of Christ we are led out of death-before-life and into life-before-death, and our world is preserved against collapse into apathy.

2
Community with Others

In a word, accept one another as Christ accepted us, to the glory
of God . . . And may the God of hope fill you with all joy and
peace by your faith in him, until, by the power of the Holy
Spirit, you overflow with hope.
— Romans 15:7,13 (NEB)

When others look at us in a friendly way, we feel alive and
vital. When others recognize us just the way we are, we feel
fulfilled. And when we feel accepted and affirmed, we are
happy, for we human beings need acceptance just as the birds
need air and the fish water. Acceptance is the atmosphere of
humanity. Where acceptance is lacking, the air becomes thin,
our breathing falters, and we languish. Therefore we are
repulsed by the indifferent glance, hurt by disregard, and
humanly destroyed when others deny us.

It is, of course, relatively easy for us to accept each other
when the others are just like us and want what we want. But it
is a different matter to accept others when they are different
from us and want something other than we do. "Accept one
another." As Paul wrote these words he had in mind the Christian congregation in Rome which was composed of Jews and
Gentiles. Of course, the Jewish Christians were already in the
minority, and the congregation continued to grow with gentile
Christians. But in their high self-esteem the Jewish Christians
viewed themselves as the true believers and older brothers. Did
they accept the gentile Christians only as "second-class Christians"? In any case, Paul, the Jewish Christian, explains to his
kinsmen: By accepting us Jews in Christ, God is showing that
he has compassion for the Gentiles. For the new hope that is

27

overflowing in us is no Jewish privilege but grace for all, without presuppositions and conditions.

In our time gentile Christianity is certainly not our problem. If Paul were to speak to us today, he would probably have to say precisely the opposite of what he said to the Romans. In his time Paul sought the community composed of Jews and Gentiles. If we gentile Christians are committed to the same thing we must seek community between Gentiles and Jews. But precisely here we run up against one of the limits of our acceptance. The Christian and political anti-Semitism of our German past have projected an image of the Jew as the scum of humanity. It began with the boycott: "A German does not buy from a Jew" and was followed by the accusation: "Judah is to blame for everything." It ended with Auschwitz. We know where that led the Jews and ourselves. Whoever is not accepted is soon expelled and finally exterminated. Unfortunately, that is not only a matter of the distant past. The terrifying United Nations' declaration on racism-Zionism is a sign that Auschwitz can be repeated today on a world scale. No matter which political solution is found in the Near East, the solidarity of Christians with Jews is now urgent. If Jews become isolated and suffer today, then we Christians must also become isolated and suffer or else become guilty. Will we find courage for accepting the Jews and for solidarity with Israel, or are these only pious words which fade away with the next oil crisis?

"Accept one another." There are persons among us who, as we say, "we like to have around." There are others who are "only tolerated." In our healthy, efficient, and achievement-oriented society, the ones whose presence is merely tolerated are the mentally and physically handicapped. Their destiny is constantly denigrated as an "existence which is merely endured." They are not ever "happily tolerated." In addition to their handicaps they are hindered by our defense reactions. The social consequences of their disability, namely our reactions to them, are worse than their handicap itself. The real disability is not a medical ailment, emotional disturbance, or physical handicap, but rather human isolation and rejection in one's environment, over-protection by parents, and insufficient help in schooling and vocational training.

Why is that so? We persons who are not handicapped naturally sense some anxiety when we first encounter a handicapped person. We feel insecure and uncertain of ourselves. It is very difficult for us to see in the handicapped person a human being who stands over against us. We see only the deformity, and we are disturbed by it. For we would like to recognize only ourselves in the other. This defense reaction reduces handicapped persons in our surroundings to the status of outcasts. They become isolated. They are overlooked or are made miserable through our sympathy. The handicapped are not our problem. We are their problem. Only when we nonhandicapped no longer represent a problem for the handicapped can their practical problems be solved through our common efforts. Where do we find the power for accepting them and for entering into community with them?

"Accept one another." Even in the church what hurts most is our lack of human relationships. The worship services in which we participate every Sunday morning themselves remain devoid of genuine human contact. We scarcely know each other with any genuine mutuality. We do not even consider it very valuable to create community with each other. "Life is lonely. No person knows the others. Everyone is alone." Is this the case even in the church of Christ? Such loneliness is intolerable.

Of course we find occasions to associate with groups in the congregation. But these relationships also cease when we leave the meeting at the church or shut our door after the meeting at our home. Can things continue to exist in this way? Can there be a preaching church in which one receives something, without a community in which one gives something?

What is the reason for this alienation from each other in which we allow others to suffer and in which we ourselves also finally suffer? The reason is that we accept others, even our neighbors, only on our own turf and view them only with our own preconceptions. And thus we do not at all seek the other but only ourselves in the other. We leave the other alone and remain alone ourselves. A further reason can be found in the fact that we accept and treat each other only in terms of reciprocity: "you scratch my back and I'll scratch yours."

There is an old principle for human community which was already stated by Aristotle: "Birds of a feather flock together." To be sure, this kind of sociality combines human beings with one another, but only human beings who are alike: whites with whites, Christians with Christians, healthy with healthy, students with students, professors with their colleagues. To those who are "in," this seems to be the most natural thing in the world. But those on the "outside" feel excluded, degraded, and wounded. We get in a stew about showing special care for those people who are included in our own circle—and then we "stew in our own juices."

"Birds of a feather flock together." But why? People who are like us, who think the same thoughts, who have the same things, and who want the same things confirm us. However, people who are different from us, that is, people whose thoughts, feelings, and desires are different from ours, make us feel insecure. We therefore love those who are like us and we shun those who are different from us. And when these others live in our midst expressing their need for recognition, interest, and humanity, we react with defensiveness, increased self-confirmation, anxiety, and disparagement. This anxiety is indeed the root of racism, anti-Semitism, the handicapping of the handicapped, and not least of all, the lack of relationships in the congregation. "Birds of a feather flock together": that is nothing other than the social form of self-justification and the expression of anxiety. This form of self-justification, therefore, never appears without aggressions against that which threatens its security. It has no self-confidence. It has no ego-strength.

"Accept one another." As we have seen, this imperative unfortunately has its limitations. The roots of these limitations lie deep within ourselves. They appear in our anxiety about ourselves, and then in the self-justification which is so deeply ingrained in us.

Accept one another "as Christ has accepted you." Only this attitude can give us a new orientation and break through our limitations so that we can spring over our narrow shadows. It opens us up for others as they really are so that we gain a longing for and an interest in them. As a result of this we become able actually to forget ourselves and to focus on the way Christ has accepted us. How have we been accepted in Christ?

To say it quite simply: God suffers because of us, for he wants to suffer us.* This is more than a word play. Indeed, everything may be at stake in this saying: he wants to suffer us, and we are indeed suffered by him. Can we suffer those who are different from us? May the others suffer us? Can we suffer ourselves? Whom can we "not endure"? We are always causing suffering for each other: siblings, husbands and wives, parents and children, neighbors and colleagues. These spheres of suffering are deeply implicated in the church and politics. If we ourselves are not able to suffer, then nothing can possibly please us. But if we are able to suffer, then we take nothing amiss. The love of God which is infinitely capable of suffering reaches us in Christ. His love is passion: passion for human beings and their worth, passion for the creation and its peace. Through his suffering because of us and through his death for us Christ has accepted us and brought us to the glory of God. We must again and again become deeply absorbed in the passion of Christ if we are to know that he suffers because of us, for he wants to suffer us. In the depths of his suffering we perceive the greatness of his passion for us. We are disarmed whenever we recognize the suffering of God which has borne and still bears his passion to us.

We are freed from the cramped life of self-confirmation. We lose anxiety about ourselves and become open for others. Prejudices fall from us as scales from our eyes. We become alert and interested, we share in life and give a share of life. Then we no longer feel that we are made insecure by others because we no longer need self-confirmation. The person who is different becomes for us, precisely because of that difference, a surprise which we gladly accept. We can mutually accept each other because Christ has accepted us to the glory of God. And because he has already accepted the others and

---

*[On the author's usage of the word "suffer" see above, p. 16, in the Introduction — Trans.]

us, the whole vista of life is opened wide before us. We stand on firm ground wherever we accept, recognize, and confirm each other. We cannot go far enough. In view of the life that has been passionately confirmed and accepted by God, there is no longer any worthless life, no "second-class" citizens. The suffering of his love has changed everything, and the more we go outside of ourselves, the more we will discover and experience this change ourselves.

If God wants so much to suffer us that he so deeply suffers for us, because of us, and with us, then we also become free to be transformed. We are not forced to hold fast to ourselves or to our image and appearance. We are already held. Since we can no longer lose ourselves, we can therefore open up and change ourselves.

No one has to nail the others down to their deeds or misdeeds. We can bear the others without image or prejudice, liberate them, and actually be present with them. Freedom and the future of God are wide open to us in the community of Christ. Thus, we can mutually free each other and hold the future open for each other. Because, as Jesus has shown us, God has pleasure in us, he puts up with very much as we daily go about making our right and wrong choices. The same also applies to our relationships in community. We can put up with differences, conflicts, and criticisms because we have found abiding pleasure in each other.

With all of our rough edges and unagreeable dispositions, we are acknowledged by Christ, brought to the glory of God, and loved with passion. If this were not true, then who would we be—a leaf in the wind, a particle of dust on the street? But if it is true that we are loved with God's passion—and I believe that this is more certain than we think—then who are we?

We are no longer individualists but a congregation in which the one accepts the other in the way that one has already been accepted by Christ. The old and very bleak principle, "Birds of a feather flock together" is then no longer valid. Instead, people who are radically different take pleasure in and accept each other. *Christian* (and this means liberating) community, then, no longer means only to sit next to those with whom I agree but also to sit next to those with whom I do not agree. Functioning with this meaning of community, we would no longer come together in order to confirm for each other the eternally same stories, jokes, and opinions, but would rather create an open and hospitable community which would bring friendliness into the unfriendly corners of this society.

Congregation, then, is no longer the sum of all those who are registered as members on the church rolls. Congregation is rather a new kind of living together for human beings that affirms:

— that no one is alone with his or her problems,
— that no one has to conceal his or her disabilities,
— that there are not some who have the say and others who have nothing to say,
— that neither the old nor the little ones are isolated,
— that one bears the other even when it is unpleasant and there is no agreement, and
— that, finally, the one can also at times leave the other in peace when the other needs it.

Does this open congregation of acceptance exist? We would be in a terrible situation if it stood before us only as a biblically based demand. If we open our eyes, we can also experience it in the power of the Spirit in our very midst. Whoever seeks finds!

In many churches today where there is much preaching but little community there are arising groups which seek community even at the expense of privacy. To that end they even open their own homes. "Grass-roots" and integrated congregations are already in existence. One need make only a small effort to seek them out. There are remedies against the sickness of a private kind of Christianity-without-commitment. Such communities are quite visible, for whoever cannot be seen cannot be accepted either. They are open communities in which everyone may participate. In those communities many persons find healing for the suffering society has inflicted upon them. The healing of the sick is a ministry in their midst. They are communities that eat and drink before open doors so that everyone can eat and drink with them. They are voluntary communities that allow for individual initiative, so that individuals must not only listen but may also speak and expect to find a hearing.

I do not believe that the lack of human relationships in our churches can be overcome except through the building up of churches that are truly congregations. While in our preaching services table fellowship is notoriously lacking, these communities assemble regularly around the table of the Lord. For the great hour of worship on Sunday morning they create the feast of the congregational gathering.

It is to be lamented, however, that society and church often do not recognize these new communities but mistrustfully repress them. The conditions where I live are similar to those in many other university towns around the world. It is extremely difficult for a single student to find a room in my home town, but when a whole community of students looks for a place to live, it usually encounters refusal on all sides. And when such communities engage in particular tasks for those who in our midst live on the periphery of society, such as handicapped people, ex-convicts, drug addicts, and people who are politically isolated, their reception is even more dubious. Whoever eats and drinks with "sinners and tax collectors" is easily compromised and stamped as a "friend of sinners." Struggling to accept those who have been denied often brings one more denial than help.

However, let us make an end, at least in the church, to discrimination against student congregations, communities who live together, and action groups! We must begin with acceptance in order to realize this goal. Counseling and criticism must continue to be given when called for, but it may not turn into malicious denunciation and official deprivation of others' rights to live.

There is in our midst, to be sure, handicapping of the handicapped, but there are also communities embracing both nonhandicapped and handicapped which create courage for life. I am not referring to helping gestures made in the direction of the handicapped, but to the communities comprised of handicapped and nonhandicapped persons living together.

Whoever has vital interest in these communities can at any time easily find out about access to them. It is not impossible to overcome those vicious circles in which anxiety among the healthy and fear among the handicapped feed upon each other. These fears and anxieties can vanish like an evil specter if practicable ways to acceptance and community are demonstrated and lived out in full view of those who are insecure.

To mention one example, in a recent summer twenty physically handicapped persons and twenty nonhandicapped persons, who had been brought together by the Protestant Youth Work of Württemberg, took a vacation together to Langeoog, an island off the German coast in the North Sea. The group had decided to demonstrate at the seaside resort, if necessary, in order to make clear to the vacationers that here were human beings who have the right to bathe on the same beach with the "beautiful" suntanned people. The demonstration was not necessary. The way in which this group swam together, played and danced together in wheelchairs in the beach house was so contagious that the vacationers spontaneously joined in. An exceptional situation? Certainly, but it shows that such community is happening.

A closed human being no longer has any hope. Such a person is full of anxiety. A closed society no longer has any future. It kills the hope for life of those who stand on its periphery, and then it finally destroys itself. Hope is lived, and it comes alive, when we go outside of ourselves and, in joy and pain, take part in the lives of others. It becomes concrete in open community with others. God has accepted us. He has hopes for us. In spite of all the intimidations of our lives, he keeps us alive and gives us courage to be. Therefore, let us impartially accept one another and hope for one another so that we mutually keep each other alive and invested with the courage to live.

May the God of hope fill you with all joy and peace in faith: you who move toward each other, you who accept each other and take pleasure in each other, you who suffer your denial in order to accept those who are denied.

Become richer in hope through the power of the Spirit, you

who bring community to the isolated ones in the forsaken corners of this society, you who live with the handicapped, the exconvicts, and the drug addicts. This is a real experience: The hope of the Spirit is given to us for the sake of the hopeless, and hope becomes certain to us in community with them. We are accepted in Christ in order that we might accept others, and the more determined we are in our accepting the more certain we are of our own acceptance.

3
Messianic Lifestyle

THE MEANING OF LIFE AND THE
STYLE OF LIFE

In everyone's life there is a correspondence between the meaning of life which one has found and the style of life which one conducts. When we experience the meaning of our life and adhere to it, we develop a personal lifestyle. We seek to orient our life to this meaning. We consciously take hold of our life and direct it by seeking to make it correspond to this meaning within changing situations and demands. The meaning of life gives us a strong heart and this in turn shapes our external way of being in the world. A meaningful life assumes a format. Personality comes into being in the reciprocity of person and history. The person attains a profile in the reciprocity between receiving and giving, between suffering and acting.

In the rapid changes of our culture and in the personal crises of our lives, however, the lifestyles to which we have become accustomed have fallen apart. Generation gaps arise. Our children call our lifestyles into question and we do not yet understand the new lifestyles which they develop. No lifestyle is valid for all times and all generations. Every lifestyle has its own time and its own term. Every life crisis is always also a crisis of lifestyle. During such crises we note that our modes of life up to this point in time can no longer assimilate and express the new experiences which we are having. We feel that we no longer know what we should do. We lose our orientation. Then a new lifestyle must be worked through, for no person can live without style, formless. One can, as the Chinese say, "lose face," but one cannot live without a face.

The Christian lifestyle is characterized and shaped by the gospel. "Let the manner of your life be worthy of the gospel of Christ," says Paul in Philippians 1:27. The life of the Christian is messianically qualified by the gospel, for the gospel is the call into the freedom of the messianic time. The Christian lifestyle therefore will be evangelical and not legalistic. That is a decisive difference.

Life under the law is principally determined by prohibitions and restraints. If one understands the Christian lifestyle legalistically, then a Christian is a person who is not allowed to do this and that, perhaps smoke, or drink, or dance. Living under the law gives us a constant fear of ourselves and anxiety before our impulses and wishes. It makes us have the gnawing feeling that we must and ought to be someone other than who we really are. Life under the law is a repressed, agonizing life. A common law demands uniformity. Everybody must either do or abstain from the same thing. When the Christian lifestyle becomes legalistic, then the Christian life becomes anxious and narrow-minded.

A life which is worthy of the gospel, however, liberates us to be ourselves and fills us with the powers of the Spirit. We are enabled to give ourselves up and trust ourselves to the leading of the Spirit. Then we are able to accept ourselves just as we are, with our possibilities and limitations, and thereby gain a new spontaneity. We are freed to live with God in the covenant of freedom. The life worthy of the gospel also has its discipline, but it is the discipline of love and joy, not the discipline of anxiety under the threat of the law.

Since New Testament times Christian piety has often been depicted with the symbol of the Christian soldier: "Onward Christian Soldiers!" Whether this symbol is helpful or not depends on the experiences we have had as soldiers. My experiences as a soldier were not very positive. Therefore I would like to employ another symbol: Christians are "artists" and their art is their life. But their life in turn is the expression of their faith and of their experiences of the Spirit of Christ. Christian life is, as theology in former times occasionally said, the *ars Deo vivendi,* the art of living with God for God. We are thus "artists of life" and we are called individually and communally to shape our life into an artwork which brings to expression something of the beauty of the divine grace and the freedom of the divine love.

Note well, we do not ourselves make this artwork. Under the law we ourselves must direct and make our life. But in the life which is worthy of the gospel Another leads us and works on us. Thus we Christians pray with Christ: "Not my will but yours be done," and we trust ourselves to the Spirit of God. Where the Christian life is concerned it is not a matter of our becoming masters through believing that "practice makes perfect"; what happens is rather that in and through our openness and our suffering God becomes our master. Often enough he leads us where we do not want to go and breaks the form of our lives which has been pleasing to us so that his form may come to expression. This is what is meant when it is said that the human being is destined to be the "image" of the invisible God on earth.

REBIRTH TO A LIVELY HOPE

Before we get into the question of the Christian lifestyle today it is helpful to take a look at the theological concept of rebirth. *Regeneratio* and *renovatio* mean that a new life is beginning in the midst of the old life.

The New Testament, however, seldom uses the word rebirth. Matthew 19:28 speaks of the "rebirth" and renewal of the whole creation in the future of the Son of man and his kingdom of glory. That is a universal and cosmic hope. Titus 3:5 speaks of the rebirth of the faithful by virture of the mercy of God through Jesus Christ "in the Holy Spirit." This rebirth of the human being happens already now "in the Holy Spirit." Those who are reborn are already becoming heirs of eternal life "in hope." The universal and cosmic expectations of the rebirth of the whole world according to Matthew 19:28 is, according to Titus 3:5, already experienced now by the faithful in their own life in the Spirit.

The First Letter of Peter praises God the Father of our Lord Jesus Christ, for "by his great mercy we have been born anew to a living hope through the resurrection of Jesus Christ from the dead" (1 Peter 1:3). Thus in the rebirth of an individual personal life nothing less than the rebirth of the whole world is experienced and anticipated. Therefore the new life of the reborn is defined by hope. In his mercy which is coming toward us God is beginning the new creation of the world into the kingdom of his glory already now in individual human beings and in the congregation through the gifts of the Holy Spirit. And this Spirit is nothing other than the power of that new creation. Where he is at work, there the process of the rebirth of the world is beginning.

Whoever is reborn in the Spirit lives in hope in the coming glory. But such a person lives in the world and with the world and for the world which shall become the theater of God's glory. For this reason anyone who is reborn cannot be anxiously preoccupied with himself or herself. Rebirth in the Spirit does not isolate us but brings us into community with other human beings. It places us in the communal movement of the Holy Spirit which will be "poured out on all flesh."

The rebirth in the Spirit thus combines a small, limited, and in itself insignificant human life with the promise of God for the whole world and thereby gives our transitory life an eternal meaning. Our life is a fragment, naturally, a fragment of death. The life which is reborn to a living hope also remains a fragment. But it now becomes a fragment of the coming beauty of the kingdom of God. Death is not the end of life in the Spirit. This life will be fulfilled in the new creation. Thus with the fragmentary life in the Spirit there is already beginning now the eternal life in the midst of a life which is leading to death. The Christian lifestyle is born out of this certainty. In living community with the Messiah Jesus, the small, incomplete human life becomes the messianic sign of the coming fulfillment of history.

CREATIVE TENSIONS

The style of a life which is reborn to a lively hope always arises in history out of tensions and conflicts. There were earlier times in which Christians could bring these tensions into a harmonious form. People developed a persistent and consistent form of Christian life; they knew how one could live in a Christian way and die in a Christian way. Calvin and Ignatius of Loyola were Christians with an impressive, consistent lifestyle. John Wesley's life is an example of the life of a consistent preacher of the gospel. But such a life is a special gift of grace. It is not always possible. Martin Luther was a person with violent inner tensions, temptations, and conflicts. He also lived in a tumultous transitional time between religious and social revolutions. His life remained a fragment.

Earlier in our villages persons were deeply rooted in the earth and in faith. They knew what in the crises of life one had to do and what one had to leave undone. Today many of us live as what Vance Packard has called a "nation of strangers," without roots, isolated in big cities. We live in a society of rapid social, cultural, and moral change. Therefore we are constantly faced with new problems for which there are no valid answers in our traditions. We live more fragmentarily and experimentally than our fathers and mothers did. We live, as it were, no longer in cathedrals but in tents. Our life story is not a long novel but rather a short story. We no longer manage comprehensive theological systems but rather topical essays. In such a time the Christian life also stands in hard tensions which often lead to disharmonies and inconsistencies. The lively hope appears more frequently at the breaking points of life than at the consistent unity of the whole.

Thus it seems to me better to make clear for oneself the tensions into which the life worthy of the gospel is led than to be on the lookout for a great, harmonious ideal for life. I mean by this the tensions between prayer and faithfulness to the earth, between meditation and political action, and between the piety of transcendence and the piety of solidarity. When we endure these tensions, when we faithfully persevere through these tensions, then the fragments of our life will also begin to be illuminated and will become signs of the lively hope.

Prayer and Faithfulness to the Earth

The dialectical unity of prayer and faithfulness to the earth was the fascinating mystery of Dietrich Bonhoeffer's piety. His *Letters and Papers from Prison*—published originally under the tension-filled title that in German meant "Resistance and Surrender"*—has become the breviary of many devoutly active Christians throughout the world. Bonhoeffer passionately struggled against the world-denying piety of those who can come to terms with every injustice on earth because basically they gave up long ago and resigned themselves to living life here only half-heartedly. But just as passionately he also resisted the banal secularity of modern human beings who, wanting to enjoy only their present, give up on the future and therefore also live only half-heartedly and without passion for other human beings. The orientation to the beyond which wants to have God without his kingdom, and the salvation of the soul without the new earth, ends up basically only in establishing an orientation to this world which builds its kingdom without God and wants to have the new earth without a new heaven. The worldless God of the one and the godless world of the other, the faith without hope of the one and the hope without faith of the other, mutually confirm each other. But in this split the Christian faith is corrupted and ruined.

"Only he who loves the earth and God in the same breath can believe in the kingdom of God," said Bonhoeffer already in 1932.† Christ does not lead human beings into remote places of religious world-flight but gives them back to the earth as its true sons and daughters. Those who really hope in the kingdom of God persevere to the end through the conflicts of their life and in the defeats of their society. They remain true to the earth and do not give up on it. Why not? Because their sight is steadfastly set upon that point where the flight from the world is broken through and God's unconditional Yes to the world is recognized, namely the resurrection of Christ. Bonhoeffer's love for the world and his hope which led him into political resistance against Hitler were totally defined by the present power of Christ through which Christ gave up his life and was resurrected from death on the cross.

We take up Bonhoeffer's starting point and develop it further when we say: The community with Christ always leads us deeper into suffering with humanity. The more intensely one loves the earth, the more acute is one's sensitivity to the in-

justice which human beings inflict on each other, to their for-
sakenness and their self-destruction. Love makes the suffering
of the other unbearable for the one who loves. One cannot
"get used to" the fact that in our big cities crime in the streets
is increasing. One can no longer stand by and simply "look on"
at the filth of the slums.

If love leads us into suffering, it also leads us into prayer.
We complain with those who must bear up under suffering
and we cry out with those who are wounded by the conditions
of their lives. What does praying mean other than to cry out to
God the complaint of those who are forsaken, the cry of those
who are oppressed, and the silence of those who are despair-
ing! On the other hand it is also true that the more spontaneously and passionately we pray the deeper we will be
drawn into the suffering of the people and participate in the
suffering of God in the world. Therefore prayer in the Spirit
and interest in life mutually stimulate, empower, and deepen
each other. Thus prayer does not compensate for a disappointed love but rather makes love ready to accept pain and to
love even more intensely than before. Faithfulness to the earth
does not dispense with prayer but only strengthens the passion
of the Spirit.

Bonhoeffer's life, his resistance, his hope, and finally his
death are an example of that lifestyle which is lived in the field
of tensions between praying and remaining faithful to the
earth. His life remained a fragment. His life was broken off in
1945 on the gallows of a concentration camp. But as a fragment it continues to illuminate and to point beyond itself.
From him we learn that the Christian lifestyle is stamped by
the acceptance of the suffering of this world. Christian life is
seldom recognizable otherwise, for "as the dying, behold we
live" (2 Cor. 6:9).

Contemplation and Political Action

The dynamic unity of contemplation and political effort for
justice in the world is the secret of the lifestyle of the Protestant
community of Taizé, in Southern France, which yearly at-
tracts thousands of young people from all over the world. At
Taizé prayer is neither a mode of inner self-reassurance nor a

religious flight from the world. It is understood in a messianic light: "Prayer is in the first instance waiting, expecting. It means to let rise day by day in oneself the 'Come Lord Jesus' of the Book of Revelation: Come for humanity, come for me."* Whoever prays in this way takes up the cry of hunger in the world. Whoever prays in this way remains in the hope of Christ. Such persons become open to the need of the world and to the future of Christ; they bind the two together in one person within themselves.

Contemplation belongs to prayer, but it is not exhausted by it nor identical with it. In contemplation, complaining ceases. The heart opens itself for reception. We become free from our self-serving desires and also from the ideals that we have for others, for our children, or for society. We listen and wait for the voice of God. Prayers without hearing and speaking with God, without waiting for God, do not lead very far. For this reason contemplation is important. It is not in itself practical, it is utterly "impractical." Yet our meditation on Christ's passion and our contemplation of his spiritual presence can alter our praxis more radically than all the other alternatives which even the most active among us can conceive. In contemplation we ourselves become another. We experience the conversion of our life and live the pains and joys of our rebirth.

A "transcendental meditation" without an object can only lead to flight from life, if not to a psychiatric clinic. *Christian* meditation is not transcendental; it is at the core always meditation on the crucified Christ in light of his resurrection. It has Christ as its "object"; it encounters him as one who stands over against the meditator. What kind of knowledge do we gain through meditation? When we wish to know something with modern scientific method we know in order to dominate or control, that is, we appropriate the object. In meditation exactly the reverse occurs: We do not appropriate Christ for our use, but we give ourselves over to Christ for his kingdom. We do not change him, but he changes us. We do not "grasp" him, but he grasps us.

What is at stake can become clear if we realize that we do not think only with the "little gray cells" of our brain. We also think with our senses. The Greek philosophers, the church fathers, and the old monastic mystics thought with the *eyes*. They were "theorizing" in the literal sense. True recognition happens only if one looks at a flower or a sunset or God until this flower is *the* flower and this sunset is *the* sunset and God is totally God. True knowing happens when the knower himself or herself becomes a part of the flower, the sunset, or God. And if one understands the subject, one says: "I see it. I see you. I see God." The result then is pure *theory*.

Today we think—at least in the German language—with our hands. We *begreifen*, we grasp. This means that we gain knowledge with the grasping, occupying, and dominating hand. And with our hands we make out of the things we grasp what we want. If one has understood a thing, one says: "I've grasped it. I've got it. I have it." The result is not pure theory but pure *domination*. When we compare these two ways of recognition and understanding we can easily see how much we modern "graspers" of everything need at least a balance between meditation and domination, between recognizing and grasping. If we ourselves are the object of the one or the other, I believe we would prefer to be "seen" and recognized than to be grasped and dominated.

If Christian meditation has this direction, then the turning to Christ and the turning to the people, for whose liberation and salvation he died, belong together as a single movement. Just as meditation must not become a flight from praxis, praxis must not be a flight from meditation. Persons who plunge into praxis because they have not come to terms with themselves prove only a burden to others. Praxis and political involvement are not cures for ego-weakness. Only those who have found themselves can give themselves. Only as I know the meaning of life can I act meaningfully for others. Only as I have become free can I free others without subjecting them to the new authoritarianism of my own ideals. Christian meditation and contemplation lead us to discover our own self as a self accepted, freed, and redeemed by God in the comprehensive context of his history with the world. When we meditate upon Christ's history and through the Spirit experience our own history with Christ, we find not only ourselves, but also our place and our personal tasks within God's history with the world.

Meditation and liberating love for the various realms of life complement each other and lead us even more deeply into the community of Christ. The Christian lifestyle arises in the field of tension between the silence of contemplation and the struggle of love for the life and freedom of others. In this field of tensions there emerge fragments, breaks, and often inconsistencies, but they point beyond themselves. The new life is seldom experienced other than as "afflicted in every way, but not crushed; perplexed, but not driven to despair" (2 Cor. 4:8).

The Piety of Transcendence and the Piety of Solidarity

These two forms of piety and of passionate interest have today polarized many groups within Christianity. There are the "new charismatic movements" and there are "Christians for Socialism." But something is being torn asunder here which in authentic Christian life must be held together: faith and love. Some who pray detach themselves from politics. They are occupied with God and their own souls and do not protest against the political and social oppression in their country because they do not feel it. In this they come quite close to certain reactionary politicians and even dictators. On the other hand, those who protested publicly against the Vietnam War, racism, and the injustice of the slums often enough took leave of traditional piety and no longer prayed at all. The unforgettable picture of Martin Luther King, together with black and white proponents of civil rights, kneeling down and praying out loud on the street in face of the sheriffs' rifles, is, at least in Germany, as repellent to many pious people as to many politically involved ones. According to our deeply engraved doctrine of the two kingdoms one must always neatly separate and hold apart religion and politics. However, I do not believe that this split has done much good for either religion or politics in Germany.

The polarization of these two groups of Christians is unfortunately far from having been overcome. The pious circles in our churches still complain about the supposed "politicization of the church" by the left. They neither see nor recognize that here Christians must, according to their conscience, take political action, and are in no way "politicizing" the church, but are rather trying to "christianize" politics. When pious circles declare themselves "unpolitical," they must be reminded that whoever is silent in the face of injustice cooperates with it. Whoever wants to be "unpolitical" in a dictatorship or a racist state is in truth supporting the public injustice and the suffering of the people. Some members of these pious groups realized too late that they owed their people the political witness of the gospel during the time of the Vietnam war.

When, on the other hand, the "Christians for Socialism" fight merely for socialism and do not do it as Christians in conjunction with the proclamation of the gospel, they lose their bearings. They then lose their Christian identity and have ultimately nothing more to offer their comrades than human solidarity without their own belief, without criticism, and without new initiatives. "Christians for Socialism" must therefore also mean "Socialism for Christ and his kingdom" so that Christ becomes the criterion not only of our faith but also of our political option.

The battle between the two groups is commonly fought out as the mindless alternative of either a vertical dimension of faith or a horizontal dimension of love. When one chooses either alternative, the tension of prayer and politics, of Bible-reading and newspaper-reading, is not sustained but dissolved. What God joined together in Christ is then put asunder. And as a result both are corrupted. Transcendence is no longer the transcendence of the risen Christ, who lives in us and with us, if it does not lead to solidarity with those whom he came to free and for whose salvation he died. On the other hand, solidarity with the poor, hungry, oppressed, and imprisoned is no longer the solidarity of the Crucified One if it does not lead to the transcendence of that freedom in which he was resurrected. The piety of transcendence and the piety of solidarity are two sides of Christian life which we must hold together. If they are separated, the new life in hope is destroyed and made hopeless.

I found a moving example of the way both belong together and can be lived simultaneously when I was in Korea. I spoke there with students of Hankuk Seminary who, after torture and isolation cells, were sentenced in 1974 to ten years or more in prison because they loved their people and had worked for social justice in the slums of Seoul and for democratic freedom in the Korean press. As a result of American intervention they were released from prison in February of 1975, yet without having their rights as citizens restored. They told me: "We went into prison like scared mice and we came out like tigers. In prison, under blows and in the darkness of the cells, we experienced the presence of God. He was there. Therefore we are no longer afraid." And they really were not afraid anymore. In spite of the prohibition of the KCIA, they reported frankly all their experiences with the police and also their experiences with God. It was told of one theology student that he had baptized thirty-two fellow-prisoners during the previous winter. What we hear today of the stance of many Christians in Korea is an impressive sign of the messianic lifestyle which combines evangelization with political resistance to evil, experience of the living Christ with the community of his sufferings.

Prayer for the Spirit makes us watchful and sensitive for injustice. It leads us along the way of the cross. And under the cross we experience ever anew the overpowering presence of the living Christ. This is the piety of the community of Christ. The form of the new life is rarely manifest otherwise than that we are "always carrying in the body the death of Jesus, so that the life of Jesus may also be manifest in our bodies" (2 Cor. 4:10).

One cannot "make " the Christian lifestyle. It is created by the Spirit when we personally and in community bind our life with the life of Christ and understand our life-history as a small part of God's great history of liberating the world. The rebirth in the Spirit renders our life a fragment of the coming rebirth of the world. Our life then begins to shine, because on it the dawn of the coming day of salvation is already reflected.

Whether we can recognize this in our own life and life- experiences is not the most important thing. It is alone important that our life, our life-experiences, and their expression in speaking and remaining silent, in doing and suffering, become a messianic sign to others. That is the work of the Holy Spirit.

Christians are witnesses, witnesses of the gospel, of the love and the freedom of Christ. Christians are not judges of their fellow Christians and their contemporaries. God alone is the Judge, and we are his witnesses in his trial with the world. Are we witnesses for the accusation of other people or are we witnesses for the defense of the accused? I believe that we are witnesses only for the defense, because we are witnesses of the divine Defender who gave his life as "a ransom for many" that, free from accusation and oppression, they might live in peace with God. "Not that we lord it over your faith; we work with you for your joy," said Paul in 2 Corinthians 1:24. On this alone and on nothing else should we depend. Christians live "messianically." We speak freely, and we set free where we can, and in a world which for many is a very unenjoyable world we help in the birth of joy.

4
Open Friendship

"SOMEONE WHO LIKES YOU"

There is a charming children's poem that also speaks to "grown-ups" and to those people who think of themselves as such. It was written by Joan Walsh Anglund, and the title of the poem and the book in which it appears is *A Friend is Someone Who Likes You.*＊

This poem about friendship speaks so peacefully and impressively because it speaks about something that is there, surrounding everyone on all sides. It does not have to be produced, it cannot be possessed, rather it waits to be discovered: the boy, the girl, the cat, the wind, the tree, or the brook. It is there in the smile of someone walking past, in the play of the wind, and in the rushing of the brook. It demands nothing from you. It likes you, whether you feel like talking now or saying nothing, whether you want to be by yourself or with someone. It is this open friendship that holds the world together. It is a delicate atmosphere. You can live in it and not notice it at all. You can live in it and spoil it continually: bringing up boys and girls, chasing away cats and mice, taking apples and pears to market, and regulating brooks. Then all you hear anymore is the din of your own thoughts and your own machines, and you no longer find anyone who likes you or whom you can like.

The words come out of a children's book and yet express what "appears" to every grown-up "in childhood, but where no one has really ever been." Ernst Bloch called it "home."† It is the world of friendship, a friendlier world. As children we were conscious (one child more so, another child less so) of this world. But the more grown-up we become, the narrower becomes our circle of friends. And there come enemies. There are competitors in the struggle for scholastic accomplishments, jobs, and careers; there are rivals in love and disappointed trust. And so we grow to be more particular about our friends, more wary with our enemies, and more unconcerned about animals, brooks, and winds. We make friendships quickly in youth; with age it becomes more difficult, until we stop. We attach ourselves more infrequently, because we no longer open our hearts. And for all that, the radiance of childhood's friendly world remains in the grownup as a flicker of yearning, making one dissatisfied with one's unfriendly environment of jobs and functions, of roles and role-expectations. What is friendship?

Friendship is an unpretentious relation, for "friend" is not a designation of office, nor an exalted title, nor a function one must perform from time to time, nor a role one is supposed to play in society. Friendship is a personal relation, "someone who likes you," someone you like.

According to Immanuel Kant, friendship combines two things: affection and respect.* Friendship is more than what we otherwise call love, eros, or charity. "Mr. Keuner preferred City B to City A," we read in Brecht's *Calendar Stories*. "In City A they loved me, but in City B they were friendly to me. In City A they made themselves useful to me, but in City B they needed me. In City A they invited me to the dinner table, but in City B they invited me into the kitchen."† To combine affection with respect does not mean wanting to serve or be useful to the other person, but needing the other just as he or she is; not just at the dinner table, but in the kitchen as well.

But friendship also combines respect with affection. You may be a respected personality, enjoy awe and admiration, and still find no one "who likes you." One does not have to submit to a friend. One neither looks up to nor down at a friend. One can look a friend in the face. In friendship one experiences oneself, just as one is, readily accepted and respected in one's own freedom. When one person likes another, then the one respects the other in his or her individuality, and delights in his or her singularities as well.

Friendship is no passing feeling of affection. It combines affection with faithfulness. You can depend upon a friend. As a friend you become someone upon whom others can depend. A friend remains a friend even in misfortune, even in guilt. For between friends there rules no prejudice that defines one, and no ideal image after which one must strive. Nor is friendship an alliance for mutual advantage, as is the case with so-called business friends. Between friends there rules only the promise to walk with each other and to be there for each other, in other words, a faithfulness that has to do not with acting and possessing but with the individual person and with being.

Friendship is therefore a deep human relation that arises out of freedom, consists in mutual freedom, and preserves this freedom. It cannot be the indifferent middle-class liberality that understands nothing and excuses everything in order to have peace. We are not by nature free, but become so only when someone likes us. Friends open up to one another free space for free life. Friends are not free without each other, but only with each other. Of course that also involves being able to leave each other in peace, like a brook that lets you be in its presence without speaking when you don't want to.

Hegel called friendship "the concrete concept of freedom."* Why? Because between friends the law of reciprocation is invalidated. One trusts a friend, one confides in a friend. When necessary, one helps, without reward, but also without intruding oneself. After all, "good turns" are not "services." We need friends, but not just in times of need; we need friends above all for the sake of joy in life. We want to communicate our joy in being and to share our happy experiences with others. Sharing in another's joy without self-interest and without envy is a good turn that cannot be regarded highly enough. Shared rejoicing creates friendship. Shared suffering follows from it, so that we say: "true friendship proves itself in misfortune." It proves itself there. But it does not originate there. And it proves itself to be simple friendship, not charitable, condescending help.

Because friendship lives without compulsion or constraint, it also demands duration. In the end, the gentle power of friendship overcomes the violent force of enmity. Duration is more than the moment. Although it is, or course, possible to have fits of rage, it is not possible to be an "enemy" forever. Indeed, "Let not the sun go down upon your wrath." Thus friendship is ultimately stronger than enmity. Enduring friendship shall possess the world.

When in the case of intimate familial relationships the parent-child relationship ceases, when the parents' task of nurturing has been accomplished and the children have become independent—then friendship comes. One doesn't have to be "Papa" or say "Mamma" forever.

When in the case of social relationships the master-servant relationship is once overcome and as far as possible done away with, and one person encounters the other with friendliness—then friendship remains.

When men and women overcome the privileges and oppression that they have built up out of their sex role-assignments—then friendship springs up between them. The friend is the new person, the true person, the free person, the person who likes to be with other people.

It is clearly necessary in every social-political order for people in various functions and with various authority to be available and to work for one another. But that is justified only so long as the need exists. It is an order of need, forced upon us by our collective need. Where does the positive remain? The positive is the simple liking-to-be-with-others in unassuming friendship, because it is free of need and liberates from compulsion. The more people begin to live as friends with one another, the more superfluous will privileges and titles of power become. The more people trust one another, the less they will have to supervise one another. In other words, the positive meaning of a domination-free, classless society is found in friendship. Friendship has been called "the soul of socialism." Without this end, in fact, class and liberation struggles do not attain any human meaning, just as socialism without friendship degenerates into soulless bureaucracy. As friendship is the "soul" of a free and just society, so, on the other hand, is a society without masters and servants the "body" of friendship. No soul without a body, no body without a soul. Whoever does not hold them together will be blessed by neither friendship nor social justice.

THE FRIENDSHIP OF JESUS

The titles employed by the Christian congregation to describe the significance of Jesus are commonly called titles of dignity, and believers conceive of his work in terms of his divine "office." In the Old Testament, God's will for the nation was carried out by prophets, priests, and kings. In the same way, Christ carries out his work in God's name in the congregation as a prophet who reveals the will of God, as a priest who represents the sacrifice of reconciliation, and as a king who rules his nation. So it is that, clothed in these titles of dignity, Jesus appears to the congregation with divine authority. The titles describe his uniqueness. But they also create a distance between him and his congregation, a distance that grows still wider through a piety which reveres and worships Christ and humbles itself beneath his authority.

One could at once remark critically that all these titles come out of an authoritarian society, and that transferring symbols of state onto Christ serves only to further intensify this domination. He—the King of Kings, the Lord of Lords, the Superstar! What does that say today in a society that, though familiar with presidents and chairmen, hardly has a place any more for prophets, kings, and priests? Will not Christ's exalted titles serve only to justify worldly rulers in the political misery that they effect? This is an easy criticism to make because it misses the point. Who is it who has been called the prophet of God? Who but the derided Son of man from Nazareth, "a carpenter's son"? If he is the prophet of God, then there is an end to every pretentious prophetic posture! Who has been called the priest of God? It is the One whom the powerful sacrificed in crucifixion on Golgotha; if this sacrifice is "the priest," then who is "Reverend"? Finally, if the powerless man on the cross has all God's power, then the crowns of the mighty ones must surely lose their halos. Thus the application of the most dignified, exalted titles this society has to the crucified Son of man from Nazareth harbors an unprecedented social-critical potential. "What the state intended to be disgrace (namely the cross) is changed to the ideal," according to Hegel.* Hegel saw therein the paradox of Christian "revolution." Yet even when one understands the paradox and, in view of Christ's passion, recognizes Christ's exaltation in his humbleness, his riches in his poverty, and his omnipotence in his powerless endurance, still the distance remains. Christ stands on God's side, speaks in God's name, dies according to God's will and rules in God's love. The exalted titles express no more than what Christ does—or suffers—for a person. They do not yet describe the fellowship he brings to men and women, new fellowship with God and with their neighbors. Whether prophet, priest, or king, whether substitute or representative, that new fellowship would be described on one side alone and would be merely functional, were not another "title" included, which can be no title, the name of friend.

Though in piety this name borders always on kitsch—"Jesus is all the world to me, I want no better friend," "What a friend we have in Jesus"—such is not the case in the New Testament. There Jesus is called "friend" in only two places; though few and often overlooked, these two places are important enough.

"The Son of man has come eating and drinking; and you say, 'Behold, a glutton and a drunkard, a friend of tax collectors and sinners!' " (Luke 7:34). The name is found in Jesus' speech about John the Baptist. John the Baptist was an ascetic and a preacher of repentance who led a legalistic life. He ate no bread and drank no wine, nourishing himself rather with locusts and wild honey. He was regarded as strange on this account. Then came Jesus. Jesus accepted public sinners—plainly spoken, criminals—and was seen "in bad company." He ate and drank with disreputable people. So he was regarded as dishonorable and lawless. That is how the people of the time interpreted and described the striking outward differences between John the Baptist and Jesus.

But what about the inner motivations? The inner motivation for Jesus' striking friendship with "sinners and tax collectors" lies in his joy, his joy in God, in the future, and in human existence. That is why Jesus celebrates the messianic feast of God's kingdom with them every time he eats and drinks with them. Jesus does not bring a dry sympathy, but an inviting joy in God's kingdom to those who are "reprobates" according to the law. Jesus celebrates the kingdom of God, which he proclaims as present in their midst, in a feast. That is why he refers to the kingdom, on more than one occasion, as the eternal "marriage feast": "Enter into the joy of your master." The respect that Jesus showed the contemptible through his affection, in that he ate and drank with them, is the right of grace, the full power of acquittal. Thus Jesus combines affection with respect. He becomes the friend of sinners and tax collectors because of his joy in their common freedom — God's future.

When "respectable society" calls him a "friend of sinners and tax collectors," however, it wants only to denounce and compromise him. In keeping with the law according to which its ranks are organized, respectable society identifies people with their failings and speaks of sinners; it identifies people with their professions and speaks of tax collectors; it identifies people with their diseases and speaks of lepers and the handicapped. From this society speaks the law, which defines people always by their failings. Jesus, however, as the Son of man without this inhuman law, becomes the friend of sinful and sick persons. By forgiving their sins he restores to them their respect as men and women; by accepting lepers he makes them well. And thus he becomes their friend in the true sense of the word. The denunciatory, contemptuous name, "friend of sinners and tax collectors," unintentionally expresses the deep truth of Jesus. As friend, he reveals God's friendship to the unlikable, to those who have been treated in such unfriendly fashion. As the Son of man, he sets their oppressed humanity free. Even in our society, which calls itself "humane" or "free," this kind of human fellowship with the unrighteous and with outcasts always has something compromising about it.

According to John 15, Jesus delcares himself to be the friend of his disciples. When he calls them to himself, he calls them into a new life of friendship: "Greater love has no man than this, that a man lay down his life for his friends. You are my friends if you do what I command you." Here the image is not that of a priest bringing sacrifice. Here the sacrifice of one's own life for one's friends is the highest form of love. But love manifests itself here as friendship. When he cites friendship as the motive for Jesus' sacrificing his life John means a love that sees, that is faithful unto death. He means a knowing sacrifice for the sake of friends' lives. Through Jesus' death in friendship the disciples become friends forever, and they remain in his friendship if they follow his commandments and become friends to others.

Again according to John, Jesus' friendship for his disciples stems from his joy in God and humanity. John reports Jesus as saying shortly before: "These things I have spoken to you, that my joy may be in you, and that your joy may be full." Jesus came from the overflowing joy of God and gives his life up for the joy of the world. After that, therefore, the disciples are no longer called "pupils" or "servants," but "friends." The relation of men and women to God is no longer the dependent, obedient relation of servants to their master. Nor is it anymore the relation of human children to a heavenly Father. In the fellowship of Jesus the disciples become friends of God. In the fellowship of Jesus they no longer experience God as Lord, nor only as Father; rather they experience him in his innermost nature as Friend. For this reason, open friendship becomes the bond in their fellowship with one another, and it is their vocation in a society still dominated by masters and servants, fathers and children, teachers and pupils, superiors and subordinates.

FRIENDS OF GOD

Knowledgeable persons hearing the words "friend of God" may think of the "Friends of God from Niederrhein," the fourteenth-century mystics. But the expression has a long history behind it. It dates back, as Erik Petersen has shown, to the circle around Socrates. The truly wise are "friends of the gods" and experience the gods' friendship even if the world around them is hostile toward them. The epitaphs of exceptional men in Greece and Egypt were often ornamented with this title. Friends of the gods are "favorites of the gods." Perhaps something of that remains with us today in such expressions as "Sunday's child" or "born under a lucky star" or when we say a genius is inspired by the muses. Sober-minded Aristotle flatly refused the expression, however. According to his *Nicomachean Ethics*, friendship—*philia*—essentially unites only peers, for a friendship can be made only in reciprocity. Therefore, no free man can be the friend of a slave, just as it would be absurd for him to regard himself as the friend of the all-powerful Zeus.* Only in a closed circle of peers can there be friendship, for only "birds of a feather flock together."

Hellenic Judaism, however, was familiar with exceptions to this rule. Thus the Greek Old Testament calls Abraham "the friend of God"; Moses is called the same, and according to the Book of Jubilees, every righteous man who keeps the law will be "inscribed on the heavenly tablets as the friend of God." This is echoed in the New Testament when James writes: "Abraham believed God, and it was reckoned to him as righteousness; and he was called the friend of God" (James 2:23). As Abraham has the place of "father of the faithful" in the New Testament, he certainly has the place of leader of the multitude of the "friends of God" as well.

In classical Christianity, then, the expression *friend of God* has had two meanings. First, it was used in a narrow, exclusive sense: Abraham believed the God of the promise, and he went out from his country and lost all that he had; therefore, it is the Christian ascetics, who forsake everything and go out poor, homeless, and solitary, who are the true friends of God. Again, Moses became a friend of the God who "spoke with him face to face" on the mountain; therefore, it is those who pray, who constantly speak with God face to face, who are the true friends of God. Finally, Christ himself gave up his life for his friends; therefore, the Christian martyrs were called the true friends of God. In this narrow and exclusive sense Christians have been regarded as friends of God only under extraordinary circumstances. Indeed, at times Christianity has even been divided into three ranks: the servants of God who are the unawakened believers, the children of God who are the awakened believers, and the friends of God who consistently have faith and follow. But at the same time, a broad, inclusive formulation has always been there too; that is, that through Christ's friendship, *all* Christians have become friends of God. Where is it that this new, so disrespectfully familiar sounding relation to God in friendship is revealed?

According to Luke and John, friendship with God manifests itself especially in prayer. In their obedience under the commandments of God, men and women perceive themselves as servants of the Lord God. In their faith in the gospel of God, they see themselves as children of God the Father. But in prayer, they speak to God as his friend. The parable Luke appends to the Lord's Prayer speaks of a quite ordinary request to a friend for bread. Although it is of course inconvenient for the friend due to the lateness of the hour, he complies just the same—because he is a friend he cannot ignore the urgency of the request. Whenever prayer is made in the name of Jesus, God is called upon as friend and importuned in the name of his friendship. Again in John, the disciples' new friendship leads them to the certainty in prayer "that whatever you ask the Father in my name, he may give it to you" (John 15:16).

Request and answer are the two sides of friendship with God. And friendship with God gives prayer the certainty that it will be answered. This can be expressed more simply in the words of Karl Barth: "God listens."* There is room enough in God's all-powerful freedom for human freedom. In the world government of God there is the possibility for human impact and participation. In the form of friend-Jesus God encounters men and women as the "answering God." He calls them not only to the submissiveness of a servant, and not only to the gratitude of a child, but to the familiarity and boldness of a friend.† After obedience and faith, therefore, prayer must come to be seen as the highest expression of human freedom in God. By bringing before God the sighing and groaning out of the depths of the world, men and women call upon God's friendship for the suffering. And God shows his friendship by hearing them. Prayer and answer are what constitute human friendship with God and divine friendship with human beings. It seems to me important to place both the praying and the answering on the plane of friendship. For then it is a relation of mutual affection and of respect for freedom. It would be servile to beg without certainty of answer; that would be respect without affection. It would be childish to try to force an answer with prayer; that would be affection without respect. A friend asks out of affection, but at the same time respects the other's freedom. He trusts in God's friendship. His prayer is not a servant's desperate begging, nor is it the insistence of a demanding child. Prayer in Christ's name is the language of friendship. And the hearing in Christ's name is hearing by one "who likes you."

OPEN FRIENDSHIP

In the notion of Jesus' friendship we find a summary of what the previously used exalted titles had to say with regard to society: as prophet of God's kingdom for the poor, Jesus becomes the friend of sinners and tax collectors; as high priest he sacrifices himself for the life and salvation of others and consummates his love through his death in friendship; as the exalted lord, he liberates men and women from servitude and makes them friends of God. In theological doctrine concerning Christ's threefold office his work has always been described in highly exalted and official terms, concealing his simple friendship in the process. The corresponding official church has therefore always maintained an exalted air as well, becoming in the process a "church without fellowship." When Christ lives and works, however, as prophet of the poor, as sacrifice for the many, and as freedom-leader, then he lives and works as friend and brings about friendship. It would be well if the church, church officials, and those taken care of by them finally recalled that together they are no more and no less than a "fellowship of the friends of Jesus." In this regard, however, we must direct a final critical look today at the phenomenon of friendship.

The expression "friendship" is of course just as misleading today as the old exalted titles were. Friendship always stands in danger of becoming exclusive. That was already the case with Aristotle. When only "birds of a feather flock together," then there may well be "honor among thieves," but it need be extended no further. It is true that the Greeks eulogized friendship as the central bond of their community. Because justice remains sterile if there is no harmony among the citizens, friendship satisfies the spirit of justice and is itself the most just of all. But it can unite only peers, for it can be made only in reciprocity. Because of this peer and parity principle, the Greek ideal of friendship tended toward exclusivity.

It is not much different in our society today. Every time we come to a "social evening," we find people are alike, who feel, think, and talk the same way. When people different from one another come together, they often split apart: men with men, women with women, young people with young people. We tend toward a "closed society." Quite aside from how hurtful it is for those who remain "out in the cold," it is also terribly boring for those "inside": always the same faces, the same stories, the same dull jokes! When Emperor Joseph wanted to open Prater as a park for the people of Vienna, the nobility protested; surely he would remain among his own kind. At that, the elderly emperor responded that if that were the case he would have to spend all his remaining days and nights in the Capuchin crypt with his ancestors.

The closed circle of friendship among peers is broken in principle by Christ, not only in relation to the despised humanity of "bad society," but in relation to God. Had he abided by the peer priniciple, he would of necessity have had to stay in heaven. But his incarnation and his friendship with sinners and tax collectors breaks through the exclusive circles. For this reason Christian friendship also cannot be lived within a closed circle of the faithful and pious, of peers in other words, but only in open affection and public respect of others. Through Jesus, friendship has become an open term of proffer. It is forthcoming solidarity.

In the Old High German language *friend* and *enemy* were still public terms derived from the protection and mutual assistance pacts. Friendship was made through pacts and preserved publicly through allegiance. But with the modern separation of the private sphere of life from the public sphere, these terms came to be assigned differently. The *enemy*— the enemy of the state, the enemy of society, the enemy of the people—has remained a political term, while friendship has shifted into the private sphere and there been internalized. The friend has become a personal friend, an intimate friend, a bosom friend, and friendship has become a matter of feeling. Because the individual becomes increasingly lonely through the separation of public and private life, he or she needs friends. But they do not substantially break through his or her loneliness. They bring only a two-party loneliness. "Blessed is he who, forsaking the world without hate, holds to his bosom a friend, and with his friend delights," wrote Goethe.* That is romantic friendship in the seclusion of privacy. Jesus' friendship for his disciples, for sinners, and for tax collectors, does not know the privacy and intimacy of modern friendship. To live in his friendship today requires that the romantic notion of friendship be deprivatized. Friendship must once again receive the character of public protection of and public respect for others. Is that possible? In this world of professions, functions, and businesses, can friendship be publicly lived and proffered?

We have models. The Quakers, for example, have been calling themselves "the Society of Friends" for centuries. Their open social work in the English slums and their political fight for the abolition of slavery in the United States provide exemplary demonstrations of Jesus' open friendship.

What would it be like if Christian congregations and communities were no longer to regard themselves only as "the community of saints," or as "the congregation of the faithful," but as such a "community of friends"? Then they would have to overcome the much-lamented disconnectedness among churchgoers (ironically termed church *visitors* in German), and make it possible for a person to feel at home in their community. Then they would have to break through their unconscious and sometimes, unfortunately, also very deliberate exclusivity with respect to the "evil world" and "unbelievers," and be ready for friendship with the friendless. Then they would have to assemble in grass roots communities that would live close to the people and with the people in the friendship of Jesus.

Talk will not bring about this change from dominion to friendship and from closed society to open fellowship, particularly if the talk takes on a threatening tone of morality: that "has to" happen. It does not "have to" happen at all. It happens wherever men and women are seized by joy in God, in people, and in the world. Therefore Nietzsche's Zarathustra

taught "not the neighbor, but the friend."* It is not by sym-
pathizing with others but by rejoicing with them that they will
be won; and with them will be celebrated the "feast of the
earth." We saw how Jesus, out of that joy in God called by the
old word "gospel," became a friend. His celebration was not
only the "wedding of the soul with God," as the old hymn has
it, but the "feast of heaven and earth," namely the celebration
of that coming kingdom which will restore heaven and earth.
This celebration makes friends and brings friendships to light
everywhere. As it seems to a child, a friend is someone who
likes you. It can be absolutely anyone or anything in the world
that can accept you as you are. Open friendship transfigures
an otherwise often unpleasant world. Open friendship
prepares the ground for a friendlier world. It brings to light a
harmony with other men and women, with God, and with
creation, and overcomes discord by accepting the forsaken. It
achieves duration and is the abiding, the dependable in the
ups and downs of life.

5
The Feast of Freedom

"One has to be very coarse in order not to feel the presence of Christians and Christian values as an oppression beneath which genuine festive feelings go to the devil . . . The feast is paganism par excellence," said Friedrich Nietzsche at the end of the last century.* As a pastor's son he must have spoken out of experience. Even today one sees the festive mood often enough "go to the devil" when one takes part in a worship service.

In the United States one is asked after a worship service: Did you enjoy the service? In my country that question can only rarely be answered with a spontaneous yes. When I first heard that question in America, it struck my German sensibility as peculiar. Is religion supposed to be fun? Must one not take worship seriously, deadly seriously? Have we not learned under the thunderous word "eternity" to confess our sins and to promise to live a better life? As children we were taught "to fear God" but not "to enjoy God." We had to sit still in church and were kept under control by our parents. The solemn hour with God dare not be disturbed by anything unexpected or irregular. Thus the intention of the sermon was to defend dogmatic orthodoxy against heresies or to demand that the people be morally responsible. The worship service was certainly not designed for enjoyment. God doesn't allow any fun with him!

Later what seemed peculiar to me was my German reaction to the American question. Where is the joy of the Spirit in our worship? Where is the liberating accent of the gospel? Is not the experience of the presence of God the most joyful thing in this world? Is not Christian worship the feast of the resurrection? Why then are not our worship services liberating feasts of heaven and earth, of the body and the spirit, of the individual and the community? Why are they not "earthly pleasure in God"? Is something wrong with our worship services or is the feast still only "paganism par excellence"?

Going back in history, we find that in Europe the secular and religious feasts were driven out of public life by the Reformation, especially the Calvinistic Reformation. Puritanism and middle-class industrialization made a pact against the festive spirit. Why? The modern world of work requires life to be rationalized in terms of its goals, means, and success. There is no way to success without consistent self-discipline and self-control. One must take one's life in one's hands and make something out of it with intentionality. One is supposed to "become something"; otherwise one is nothing. For people who adapted to and accepted the discipline of modern life, games seemed like "childish things" and the liturgies of worship like "women's things." The more people came to see the meaning of their lives in terms of calculable ends, the less meaning they could see in the purposelessness of games and the uselessness of fests. Thus, for these modern people, enlightened Protestantism reduced the liturgies of Christian worship to doctrinal and moral instruction, excluding doxological and hymnological expressions as superfluous and merely time-consuming. The farmers in northern Germany used to stand outside the church on Sunday morning and chat about business, while their wives and children were singing and praying in the church. The men came in only when the sermon began. Playing was left to the children and praying to the women.

Today, however, there is a growing uneasiness with and criticism of our rationalized world of goals, means, and success—a rationalized world which increasingly seems to impoverish human life. In this world the question of a rebirth of feasts in culture, of a capacity for play in personal life, and of the power for celebration of free and open liturgies in the representation of Christian freedom and joy is acquiring new importance. When one experiences the free worship events of African independent churches and sees how they pray spontaneously and how they, as David once did before the altar, sing and dance before the Lord, one feels somewhat alienated from oneself and one's body. One is like a person with two left hands, unable to give oneself out of one's hands. This loss of spontaneity is experienced by many people today, with or without criticism of culture, as impoverishment.

Thus there is a remarkable reversal in our modern lifestyle. First we learned how to control ourselves and keep our feelings secret: "Do not let yourself go, do not express your feelings." Afterward, when we felt how poor life had become under this permanent self-conscious stress, we were advised "to relax" and given all sorts of methods for eliminating tension. First, we had to kill our feelings, and then we needed "sensitivity training" and "scream therapy" to regain them. Now, we catapult from one method into another and never know quite how to get out of this type of "methodism." We remain cool and rootless. One can learn how to deny one's urges but not how to express one's urges and affections spontaneously. For that one needs the free zone of the feast and liberation to festive life.

FUNCTIONAL ANALYSIS OF THE FEAST

Today we are used to analyzing conditions and events according to their social function. That is of course important, but it has its limitations. Functional analysis is an analysis of purposes and uses but not an analysis of the meaning itself.

Functional analysis reveals the worship service as a ritual. Before anyone in the church speaks or sings, the church has already spoken and sung through its ritual. Preachers come and go, but the ritual remains and speaks its own language. It draws religious needs and public expectations into itself. If the minister has not preached well, he or she can be consoled with the thought that the hymns were well-selected. And if the hymns were unfamiliar, being in church will still have the functions which the worshipers ascribe to it. An effective church reform begins first of all by changing the rituals. Thus there have been more splits in the church on account of rituals than on account of substantive questions or interpretations.

The ritual of the worship service is fixed. The weekly recurrence of Sunday renews time which has been used and worked through. Like the Christ child, Christmas comes "again every year" to give order to the flux of time. Through its great feasts the church year brings time into the cycle of the eternal return. This was already the case in pagan feasts. By festively repeating the eternal orgin of all things, they renewed the week, the month, the year, and the aeon. Without such rituals of time it would evidently be difficult for human beings to exist in what Mircea Eliade has called the "terrors of history."* Every ritual creates historical continuity and orders the future through memories. This is true of middle-class birthday celebrations as well as of national holidays. Without ritual there is no tradition, and without tradition there is no identity.

Every ritual furthermore stands in a social context and creates social communication. Through ritual celebrations a group assures itself of its own identity and context and portrays itself publicly. Because rituals have the power of socialization, they are bound up with sanctions against deviants and outsiders. Only those who participate are "in." Groups constitute themselves over a period of time only through symbolic interactions and thus through trusted rituals. Appropriate taboos protect groups against disturbances and intrustions. In this sense one is viewed as a "Christian" if one is a "churchgoer," "stays involved in the congregation," and practices the appropriate symbolic interactions. This means that one lays claim to those rituals which accompany and give order to the crucial passages of one's life, rituals which are viewed as meaningful and are called "official acts." One "belongs to the church" "when one allows" one's children to be baptized and confirmed, and oneself to be married and buried by the church.

Rituals of time and rituals of community always have a symbolic character. Through the binding together of two levels, the sign and the thing denoted, the ritual act becomes the symbol which points beyond itself, expresses something greater, and invites us to memory, to hope, to a new aspect of life, or to community. Through the celebrative representation, the thing represented becomes emphatically present.

It is obvious that a functional analysis can show church

ritual acts in their historical, social, and anthropological necessity. But any other religious or ideological content can invade and fill these functions. Rituals of time and rituals of community, initiation rites, and maturation ceremonies are to be found everywhere. They can be religious, but they do not have to be. They can be Christian, but they are not necessarily so.

The functional analysis of ritual looks into its necessity and understands ritual as the indispensable stabilization of life against the background of the "still undetermined animal," namely the human being as the creature who is open to the world, flooded with stimuli, and unstable. Functional analysis begins with the modern means-to-an-end rationality and notices only the official function of rituals, fests, and celebrations. The predominant question is, What is the use of it? It only too easily overlooks the superfluous, because apparently unusable meaning which especially characterizes religious rituals. In everything that human beings have to produce ritually in order to survive, they also portray themselves. They express their experiences and themselves. It is an old wisdom of the Methodist church that experience demands expression. There is no experience without the expression of the experience; there is no joy without laughing, no pain without weeping. Whenever human beings can express the experiences of their life, they show their freedom. The expression itself already has a liberating effect. Religious rituals do not have only stabilizing functions which are related to need. By expressing the basic experiences of life and of a community, they also demonstrate the value of being. Ritual is not something that is useful and functional for other purposes; it is in itself meaningful. There are also traces of this freedom in the expression of life and of the joy of life in the nonhuman creation. "Even the birds sing more than would be permitted by Darwin," said the Dutch biologist Buytendijk.* What seems externally and functionally without purpose is in principle the most meaningful possibility we have in a world of making, using, and having.

Another Dutch writer, Felix Timmermans, portrayed an unusual young man in his novel *Pallieter*. One day Pallieter was standing under a tree enjoying the brilliant sparkles of the sun reflecting on the leaves. A man, certainly a modern man, passed by and asked: "What are you doing there?" as if we must always be "asking about" and "doing something." Pallieter answered: "I am."* This is a beautiful answer. It is the answer which the joy of being gives to the stress of the modern rational world. "I am" is more than "I have." The expression of the joy and the sorrow of being is more than the pursuit of having and using everything that can be acquired. Only in that does the category of being gain the upper hand over the category of having: "I am, but I do not yet have myself" instead of "I am what I have, what I achieve, or what I can make out of myself."

Religious feasts have always shown this creative play of expression, of free self-portrayal, and this demonstrative value of existing which cannot be reckoned according to purpose and use. It is this alone which makes a ritual, beyond its necessity, into a feast. Religion is not at all what Marx referred to as "the sigh of the oppressed creature, the feeling of a heartless world."† Rather, religious rituals are the "feasts of the gods" and are celebrated with the gods. Religion can become the "opium of the people." But from the point of view of the history of religion it is better to understand it as ecstasy, orgy, and exuberance. Nietzsche was right in claiming that pagan religions were essentially festal religions. In the feast, the finite and limited human life is given the highest, because freest, expression before the infinity of the gods' world.

Today, however, this genuine festive feeling has "gone to the devil." What is the reason for this?

CRITICAL ANALYSIS OF THE FEAST

In our modern world work has deprived the religious feast of the meaning of the regeneration of life from its eternal origin. The reproduction of life through work puts a stop to the festal renewal of life from a transcendent source. Thus the modern world has ascribed wholly different functions to feasts and holidays. They are no longer the primal religious forms of expression, nor are they merely universal anthropological functions. Formally feasts and holidays now play the role of the temporal suspension of those laws and attitudes which regulate everyday work. Everyone should take a "pause," rest from the pressure of activity, relax and recuperate. What purpose does this serve?

Because the modern world of work demands functional proficience and purposeful behavior, it requires the sacrifice of repressed drives, not to speak of the exclusion of those who are not proficient. Without the opening of periodic and controlled outlets the psychic burden can become too much to bear and the necessary self-control cannot be maintained. Freedom, feasts, and celebrations thus take on the function of venting the regimented repression of emotions and aggressions. But when they function in this way they serve a domination that is not reconciled with freedom. This is true both in personal life, where spontaneity and self-control cannot be integrated, and in public life, where the people who are dominated are provided "bread and circuses" so that, having "had a ball," they may again be better regulated. This is an old rule: All forms of repressive authority must provide safety valves from time to time so that the aggression they generate in the people they rule can be safely worked off. Nowhere are political jokes so much alive as in dictatorships. It was Hitler's cynical propaganda minister, Joseph Goebbels, who recognized the venting function of these jokes: "They are the bowel movement of the soul."

Because daily life is marked by tension, stress, and pressure to achieve, it needs periodic suspensions and open vents. One needs unburdening in order to bear the burdens, and relaxation in order to endure the tensions. One must "take a vacation" in order to recover one's energy for work. One seeks in vacation a "compensation for the life of the workday." One goes to church in order "to get oneself together," "to come to oneself" again, and to reconcile oneself with the unreconciled everyday. With these reliefs and relaxations go hand in hand those compensations which make all free time a function of the nonfree time and which offer a substitute joy for the joyless life of the workaday world.

This can be called the *Coca-Cola philosophy*, which is built around the stress of the modern world. "The pause that refreshes" says that life is really constituted by work and you will not find enjoyment in the world, but there are pauses in which one is to become refreshed so that one can work even better afterwards. Therefore drink this artificial product. There are also "activities" for leisure time. Because everything depends on "keeping in shape," cities build recreation centers for their citizens and sophisticated fitness clubs are provided for the high achievers of the business world.

Christian worship on Sunday, the day without work, is no exception to what has just been described. It is used in the same way by the exhausted people of our society, even if it cannot proffer the same "leisure activities" and "fun." For many people the principal objective of worship is inner, spiritual relaxation and religious unburdening of the responsibilities they have to shoulder during the week. Not surprisingly the Christian worship service is experiencing increasing competition in this respect from the new religious modes of meditation which are ostensibly Eastern in character. In modern society the religious functions of suspension, venting, unburdening, and compensation can be taken over by Christian worship. But there is no necessity that Christian worship assume these forms. All this can happen in quite different contexts, as the "competition" now shows. Therefore the congregation must ask itself whether in fulfilling for many worshipers only this function of unburdening it is actually expressing the true joy in the freedom of Christ.

The alienation which results for those who attend our feasts, celebrations, and free periods can be broken only where people can see and accept in them a real alternative to the everyday world of work. Then they no longer serve the reproductive imagination, working off the boredom and frustration of everyday. Then they are not only a source for the recreation of our exhausted energy. Rather they become the expression of our creative imagination which investigates and explores the frontiers of future freedom. Feasts and worship must then be understood as a source for the creation of new life. In them we no longer simply play with the unreal possibilities of the present ("If I were a bird . . . "—but unfortunately I am not) but with the real possibilities of the future so that the present may become freer and more human. We do not compensate for our suffering from the lack of freedom with the dream of a freedom in another world—"Freedom," said Schiller, "exists only in dreams and beauty blooms only in poems"*—but through courage for the liberation of this world we dissolve already here and now the ban against transforming life. Insofar as they serve the functions of unburdening, venting, and compensation, feasts have a stabilizing effect for work and domination. Insofar as they serve the functions of anticipation, alternative, and experiment, feasts introduce an as yet unknown freedom into the midst of unfree life. The constraint of destiny and the impression of one's own powerlessness are broken through when the new possibilities and powers of liberation are experienced in feast and cult.

But these other functions of feast depend utterly on *what* is actually celebrated in feast and cult. Therefore we must now leave the functional as well as the critical analysis of rituals, feasts, and cults and attempt to present the substance of that freedom which is expressed in Christian worship.

THE FEAST OF THE RESURRECTION

In essence Christian worship was and is the feast of Christ's resurrection from the dead. For this reason it was celebrated on the first day of the Jewish week, on Sunday at sunrise. It was always celebrated eucharistically with bread and wine. Easter begins with a feast, for Easter is a feast and makes the life that is derived from it a festive life. "The resurrected Christ makes of life a continual feast," declared Athanasius,† and Roger Schutz has rightly placed this idea at the center of the Council of Youth at Taize. Jesus himself continually compared the rule of God which he proclaimed and lived with a "marriage feast." His earthly life was a festive, a liberating, and a redeeming life. How much more will Christianity have to understand his resurrection from the dead as the beginning of a joy which does not pass away and celebrate it with a bliss which does not fade! As the "first fruits of those who have fallen asleep" and the "pioneer of life" against the powers of death, he is the "leader of the mystic round dance" and the church is the "bride who dances with him," as Hippolytus said.* Long before the gloomy dance of death was graphically depicted in the Middle Ages, there existed in the ancient church the dance of the resurrection. The Resurrected One leads the polonaise and dances with each person into the kingdom of God—unlike death, which dances with each one into the grave. He is exalted to be not only the Lord of God's rule but also the "Lord of glory" (1 Cor. 2:8). Thus even today in the Eastern Church the "transfiguration" of Christ is the center of the hope for the transfiguration of the cosmos. The Resurrected One has an effect on the weakness and fragility of human life not only through the forgiveness of sins and his commands but even more through his beauty and glory. In the words of Dostoevsky, his "beauty will redeem the world," for experienced grace shows itself in the bodily graciousness and gracefulness of lived freedom.†

Easter is the feast of freedom in which the resurrected Christ sits at table with his disciples. Easter epiphanies and celebrations of the Lord's Supper probably belonged together originally. It is the eating and drinking in the kingdom of God which the Resurrected One anticipates with everyone whom he has made a friend. One cannot only proclaim and hear this freedom; it must be tasted. If Christian worship is essentially the feast of the resurrection, it must also be eucharistic. The feast of the resurrection and the Eucharist do not constitute a religious escapade in heaven but stand in the midst of history and combine in a singular way past and future, memory and hope. The presence of the suffering and the death of Christ is hope in the mode of memory. The presence of the coming kingdom of God is memory in the mode of hope. Through the Eucharist the death of Jesus is proclaimed until he comes, says Paul. It is at the same time the sacrament of memory and hope and, in the harmony of both, the expression of presently experienced liberation. According to Thomas of Aquinas, every eucharistically celebrated worship is a "sign of the memory of Christ's suffering and death," a "sign of hope in his future glory," and in the unity of both "a demonstration of grace."‡ These three dimensions must be held together: without hope in the kingdom the Supper becomes merely a memorial; without memory and hope it loses itself in the mystical presence of eternity.

With Easter, and thus actually in every worship service, there begins the laughter of the redeemed, the dance of the liberated, and the creative play of fantasy. Throughout the ages Easter hymns have celebrated the victory of life by laughing at death, ridiculing hell, and driving out the demons of the anxiety produced by guilt. Easter sermons in the Middle Ages are said to have begun with good jokes. In such Easter laughter there is still an unexhausted potential for attitudes of resistance. Laughter disarms a threat by taking away its seriousness. It shows unassailable freedom where the enemy had counted on anxiety and fear. When people can laugh they can no longer be threatened or blackmailed. And if the foundation of all domination and oppression of human beings is the threat of death, then the liberation of people who are in this way threatened and oppressed begins with the feast of the resurrection. This can be seen already in the first Easter hymn, 1 Corinthians 15:55-57: "Death is swallowed up in victory. O grave, where is thy victory? O death, where is thy sting?" The same notion recurs in Paul Gerhardt's Easter hymn: "The world with its great wrath is for me a laugh; it is angry but can do nothing; all work is forlorn . . ." The liberating feast of the resurrection stands between the internal and external slavery which is passing away and the unlimited joy of the coming life in freedom. In it a freedom is experienced and a joy is expressed which otherwise does not appear. It therefore takes shape in ecstasies of happiness and love which overcome distances. The "feast of freedom" cannot really be without a kind of euphoria. But it is not simply awakening a passing euphoria when it grasps human beings at the core of their real oppression and, through the freedom that they celebrate here, wakes their hunger for freedom everywhere; when it encounters human beings in their repressed feelings of loneliness and, through the community they are now celebrating, wakes their cry for the other person in daily life. Then from this feast one takes into everyday life a memory which cannot be forgotten. This memory works as a radical contrast to the normal regimented life and lets us seek possible ways of transforming it. The "liberating feast" thus builds up tension over against daily life which can be resolved only through conscious suffering from its hindrances to freedom and through conscious intervention for more freedom and more open community.

The memory of Christ's suffering and dying forbids our using the feast as an escape from the miserable conditions of the world. Rather it makes silent suffering a conscious pain. But the hope of the resurrected and coming Christ also forbids us simply to complain about suffering or simply to indict its causes. In this feast the joy in freedom is deeply bound up with pain over experienced unfreedom, for the ecstatic rejoicing leads into ever deeper solidarity with an unredeemed world (Rom. 8). Where freedom comes near, the chains begin to hurt. This dialectic of the Christian feast may not be one-sidedly abolished. It leads into the dialectic of life itself: the more lively love makes life, the more deadly is death experienced; the more one goes outside of oneself, the more vulnerable one becomes.

SABBATH AND SUNDAY

Why is the feast of the resurrection celebrated every Sunday and year after year? The one who was crucified "once for all" and was resurrected "before us"—he "will never die again" (Rom. 6:9)—breaks through the festal cycle of the eternal return. How can his feast be dated according to the orbit of the stars?

This question can be answered first with the Jewish understanding of the sabbath. The sabbath goes back to the creation story. The seventh day is the feast of creation. On that day God "rested" and took pleasure in his creation because "everything was very good." But according to the creation narratives this cannot be understood as exhausted rest after strenuous work. It is the goal of the divine creating and its fulfillment. The "good pleasure" is the quality of the divine

life. The feast of creation is also the goal of God's history with
the world, from the creation in the beginning to the creation
of the end-time. Therefore the sabbath also reaches forward to
the messianic times. The messianic time is often called the
"age of the eternal sabbath," and thus the weekly sabbath is
understood as the anticipation and foretaste of this future.

The sabbath expresses the central idea of Judaism, the idea
of freedom and of utter harmony between human beings and
between human beings and nature. This is, in the words of
Erich Fromm, "the idea of the anticipation of the messianic
time and of man's defeat of time, sadness, and death."*
Because all work is a human invasion of nature, sabbath rest
means the state of peace between human beings and nature.
The weekly sabbath is not merely ritual and symbol of the
eternal return but an anticipation of shalom, even if it happens on the "exceptional day." The sabbath of course stands in
the weekly cycle, but in its content it breaks through the
cyclical rebirth of time by anticipating the messianic time. It
stands in the cycle of time and yet is a sign of freedom from the
cycle of time, for it anticipates the victory over time and
death. "Time is," as Fromm says, "suspended; Saturn is
dethroned on his very day, Saturn's-day. Death is suspended
and life rules on the Sabbath day."†

Jesus' view of the sabbath is often reduced to his polemic
against ritualization: "The sabbath was made for man, not
man for the sabbath; so the Son of man is lord even of the sabbath" (Mark 2:27-28). This is the reason for his healing of the
sick on the sabbath. The sabbath is made for humankind's
sake, not for work's sake. Jesus does not direct the sabbath
toward the workdays. The fact that "the blind receive their
sight, the deaf hear, and the dead are raised up" is actually
part and parcel of Jesus' messianic mission. According to Luke
this begins with the proclamation of the final "acceptable year
of the Lord" through Jesus in Nazareth (Luke 4:18ff.). According to Leviticus 25 this is the "sabbatical year," and according to the prophets (Isa. 61:1ff.) it is the final dawn of the
messianic time, in other words, the fulfillment of the weekly
sabbath's anticipations and promises.

Jesus therefore, as Herbert Braun points out, did not make

the sabbath "a matter of indifference."* Like the prophets he consistently polemicized against the confining of God's history and law to the cult and to cultic seasons. He abolished the separation between the cultic and the profane, the pure and the impure, sabbath and everyday. He did this however, not in favor of everyday secularity but in favor of the messianic festiveness of the whole of life. If his mission is messianic, then with him the sabbath of the end-time also is beginning. The whole of life becomes a feast.

We know, of course, of no special pilgrimages made by Jesus to cultic festivals. But his journey to Jerusalem which ended with his passion and crucifixion can be understood in this sense as Jesus' festal procession. If the rule of God and with it the liberation of human beings are revealed in Jesus' suffering and dying, then his sacrifice must also be understood as the end of the special cult and the beginning of a new quality of life in the feast of God's rule. As the end of the special sabbath the history of Jesus is the beginning of the all-embracing and ultimate sabbath.

The Christian cult consists of Christ's person and history and of the actual history of the congregation with Christ in the Spirit. Therefore there is no special "Christian cult." Paul understood this new qualification of the whole of life through Christ and asserted it against both Judaism and enthusiasm in his congregations. The freedom for which Christ has freed us is not compatible with any cultic legalism (Gal. 5:1ff). For Paul the observance of holy days, months, and festal seasons indicated a lack of knowledge of the true God. For those who know God, all days are alike (Gal. 4:8; Col. 2:16; Rom. 14:5). "I appeal to you therefore, brethren, by the mercies of God, to present your bodies as a living sacrifice, holy and acceptable to God, which is your spiritual worship" (Rom. 12:1). If the surrender and obedience of our bodies on the ground of God's mercy, that is, Christ's sacrifice for us, is called "worship," then, as Ernst Käsemann has said, the "doctrines of worship and Christian 'ethics' converge."†

But worship is not replaced by ethics; rather ethics are made worship! The new unity of worship and life which abolishes the separation between everyday and feast day cannot be inter-

preted in the categories of ethics, of secularity, or of everyday.
The feast of God's rule is to be lived in the profanity of everyday. Bodily obedience in resistance to the powers of the passing world and its laws becomes the "offering of one's sacrifice."
The service of reconciliation in the forum of the world
becomes the expression of joy in God's rule. For this reason
worship has priority over ethics.

In the ancient church Chrysostom once gave an appropriate
new definition of festivity: "Where love is enjoyed for itself,
there is festivity."* The love which serves the neighbor without
its own purposes and motives is joy. It is the feast of the new
life. It does not need any special festal or leisure times.
Wherever it comes into being there is the sabbath, the acceptable year of God, the messianic time. To preach the gospel of
the kingdom to the poor, to heal the sick, to accept the despised, to free the prisoners, and to eat and drink with the
hungry is the festal procession of Christ in God's history with
the world.

It is understandable that John saw no temple in his visions of
the new heaven and the new earth and the Jerusalem coming
down from heaven. What the temple in the sacred zone represented, namely, the cultic indwelling of God, is superfluous if
the glory of God fills everything. Thus also for John the separation of temple and street, Sunday and everyday, is overcome
by the One for whom the temple and Sunday stand. This overcomes even the temple and Sunday.

SUGGESTIONS FOR THE FEAST

As ritual, worship is a celebration. Only a relatively closed
group with years of practice can internally carry out ceremonies and symbols which have been formed through long
tradition. But as a feast the service is closer to unsolemn, open
play.† A celebration can be disturbed merely by anything
unexpected. But the feast is open for spontaneous notions and
for accidents which come from the outside. In the feast there
are no disturbances, only surprises. It is also possible for
strangers to participate in the feast. For a feast only the broad
design is planned in advance. What happens in it is a matter

for the participants themselves. Therefore the feast widens the traditionally fixed elements of the celebration in order to allow for spontaneous and creative contributions. If we understand Christian worship messianically, we will have to broaden its celebrations with elements of the feast, and its dignified ceremonies with spontaneous festivity. Then it can have its influence on the festivity of everyday life.

The Christian worship service is originally the feast of the resurrection of Christ. The resurrection feast is a feast with the Resurrected One. It reveals and demonstrates the alternative of hope to this world of work, guilt, and death. The inevitability of history is broken through, the constraint of evil is abolished, and death is disarmed. Resurrection is festively celebrated as such an alternative, and is brought into the midst of unfree and alienated life as an anticipation. The feast of the resurrection is a festive act of resistance. Thus there is also present in it the contradiction of the powers of death that oppress life and of the apathy that surrenders to them. This disarming of the powers and the rebirth of hope out of apathy should be stressed more strongly than in the past in order to free worship from misuse as a vent and compensation. As an action of hope in the resurrection, the worship service is a critical-liberating and therefore public matter.

As the feast of the Resurrected One the Christian worship service is at the same time the making present of the One who was crucified. Together with the joy which is revealed in it, it also expresses pain over the failures and omissions of life. Where the nearness of God in the Spirit is experienced, there the godlessness of life also enters into the consciousness. Where human beings begin to live in the kingdom of the Son of man, inhuman relationships and inhuman behavior become painfully manifest. In this sense the worship service will express the people's laments in the Psalms and their cries from the depths of the assailed life. If the service is expanded from a ceremony to a feast, this cannot be accomplished through preformulated psalms and prayers, but must also happen through spontaneous laments arising from the life-situation of individuals and whole groups. The feast of the resurrection gives place for the cry of the Crucified One to God and for the outcry of the

dumb, imprisoned, and suffering people. "And if man in his
torment falls dumb, a God taught me to say how I suffer," said
Goethe.* The human, suffering, crucified God, whose presence is celebrated in the worship service, allows us to cry out
and say what we suffer. If he breaks the constraint of silence,
he will also bring to expression politically the cry of the broken
people who have been silenced. A celebration cannot bear the
unanswered cry out of the depths or the pain which finds no
balm. But the feast with the Crucified One in the presence of
the Resurrected One is open for this.

If worship in the name of the Crucified and Resurrected
One struggles against the internal and external oppressions of
life, its criticism of the world is nevertheless bound up with the
human being's justification and assent to creation. Precisely
because it is the ferment of critical liberation, it mediates the
power to accept existence. It does not justify the given state of
affairs or the conditions of domination, but it does justify creation as it originally was and ultimately will be. Throughout its
criticism of evil the feast will be an affirmation of existence
and thus also an expression of joy in that existence.† The Yes
of God's incarnation implies the No of the cross. Throughout,
the No of the cross the Yes of the kingdom is to be heard and
cannot be exchanged with any other coerced or voluntary affirmation of things that are not "very good."

The feast of the resurrection has elements of exuberance
because of the presence of the Resurrected One. The new life
is not merely a changed life, but a life with a new quality. The
exuberance of God's future will first of all be sensed and
celebrated in festive ecstasy. It can be translated into practice
only in a preliminary and fragmentary way. But the liberating
feast is not for this reason meaningless or superfluous. Precisely its "superfluity" in the literal sense calls forth constantly new
attitudes of resistance against the various forms of oppression
and unfree life. It provokes and stimulates the fellow participants, according to the powers they receive and the possibilities they recognize, to bring freedom and greater openness
into everyday life. The feast of the freedom of Christ and the
serene joy in him are not a contradiction of struggle and work
and do not paralyze energies. The spirit of the feast protects

the struggle for the liberation of the poor from ideological stringency and demonism and keeps us from resignation in the face of resistances and the impression of our own powerlessness.

The messianic feast is dependent on a community which understands itself as a messianic community. A religious church which simply takes care of the people will always understand its worship services as church "events" and stylize them as fixed ceremonies; as such they will be generally viewed as rituals with social functions, adapted to the present needs of human beings in particular social situations. But a communal church which is *of* the people will see itself as the subject of its gatherings and will form its worship into feasts of its own history with God. Reform of worship and reform of the congregation therefore belong together. There will be no reform of worship without a new formation of the congregation "from below," that is, its own organization of itself according to the promises and demands of the gospel.

Is Christianity an oppression under which the genuine festive mood "goes to the devil"? If Christianity is the faith and the practice of the resurrection, then the "genuine festive mood" has its beginning point only with Easter. Then the feast is "Christianity par excellence." Yet the rebirth to an Easter Christianity has yet to be realized.

6

The Ecumenical Church
Under the Cross

DIALOGUE *ABOUT* OR *UNDER* THE CROSS

The ecumenical movement of the divided Christian churches and confessions seeks the visible unity of the church of Christ. But where else can the churches' unity be found than in one Lord of the church and the undivided offering of his divine life upon the cross for the salvation of the world? The unity of the church can only be a unity in truth, and the truth which demands unity and makes it possible is the all-embracing and all-saving truth of his sacrificial death on the cross at Golgotha. The internal basis of the ecumenical movement is found in the priestly prayer of Christ himself: " . . . that they may be one" (John 17:21). The external basis for the communion of Christians upon earth lies in the catastrophic "sufferings of these times." Only through ecumenical communion within itself can Christianity witness the peace of God to this divided, oppressed, and disturbed world.

The internal basis takes precedence, however, over the external because the renewal, liberation, and unification of the church of Christ upon earth will result, not primarily from theological strategy and ecclesiastical tactics to draw together, but rather from the very root and wellspring of the church, namely, the power of Christ's own passion. It is in his outpoured blood and in his open heart that the church is already renewed, liberated, and one. The ecumenical movement toward the unity of the church is essentially a movement coming from the cross of its one Lord.

The way toward ecumenical agreement among the separated churches began with the effort to find a comparative ecclesiology. Mutual understanding was developed in the hope, as it was expressed at the Edinburgh conference of 1910, that "a better understanding of the divergent viewpoints about faith and order would lead to a more profound desire for reunion, and to the corresponding official decisions by the various confessions."* The result of this work, which is still far from completion, was a kind of negative consensus. It has been discovered that traditionally separate doctrines need not necessarily result in separate churches; they can also lead to mutual complementarity and enrichment. Hence, the varying theological and ecclesiastical traditions were no longer seen to require that separateness which excommunicates, even though it was not yet possible to formulate the common tradition which unites us.

Not until the Conference of the Faith and Order Commission at Lund in 1952 was the step made from comparative ecclesiologies to a christological ecclesiology:

> We have seen clearly that we can make no real advance towards unity if we only compare our several conceptions of the nature of the Church and the traditions in which they are embodied. But once again it has been proved true that as we seek to draw closer to Christ we come closer to each other. We need, therefore, to penetrate behind our divisions to a deeper and richer understanding of the mystery of the God-given union of Christ with His Church.†

This movement from a purely external comparison of ecclesiologies to an inwardly binding, christological ecclesiology has since then characterized the process of ecumenism: the nearer we come to Christ, the nearer we come to each other.

The ecumenical dialogue about the meaning of Christ's cross began in the same way. The paschal mystery, the eucharistic truth of the cross, experiences deriving from the spirituality and the suffering of the cross, and the Protestant theology of the cross were analyzed and compared. The result was a richer and deeper understanding of the passion of God and the liberating strength that comes from discipleship with the Crucified One. But this fruitful dialogue *about* the cross of Christ would remain abstract and merely theoretical if it did not at the same time lead to a dialogue *under* the cross of

Christ. This is the case because the cross is not just one object among others or something about which we may speak objectively. Christ's cross is the place where we are assembled and made more deeply one than we could ever have conceived. Hence, no dialogue *about* the cross is possible without standing together *under* the cross, and no ecumenical discussion about church unity is possible without the liberating discovery of the church's unity within the self-offering of Jesus Christ for the salvation of the divided world. But this means that the nearer we come to the cross of Christ, the nearer we come to each other.

Ecumenism does not come into existence because of a human vision of unity, albeit such a utopia of peace is important in view of the threatened destruction of humanity because of its divisions. Basically, it is not unity which brings salvation, but salvation which brings unity. Ecumenism does not derive from Christian power-politics vis-à-vis the state and secular society, even though there is also validity for the churches in the motto: "united we stand, divided we fall." The true Christian quality leading to unity is not the love of power, but the power of love.

Ecumenism comes into being wherever—and this is everywhere—we find ourselves under the cross of Christ and there recognize each other as brothers and sisters who are hungry in the same poverty (Rom. 3:23) and imprisoned in the selfsame sin. Under the cross we all stand empty-handed. We have nothing to offer except the burden of our guilt and the emptiness of our hearts. We do not stand under the cross as Protestants, as Catholics, or as adherents to Orthodoxy. Here, rather, is where the godless are justified, enemies are reconciled, prisoners are set free, the poor are enriched, and the sad are filled with hope. We discover ourselves, therefore, under the cross both as children of the same freedom of Christ and as friends in the same fellowship of the Spirit.

The nearer we come to Christ's cross, the nearer we come to each other. How can our divisions and our enmities be maintained in the sight of his bitter suffering and death? How, in the light of Christ's "open heart," can we remain closed and be fearful about the church? And how can we, grasped by the outstretched arms of the suffering God upon the cross, clench our fists or with unrelenting fingers hold fast to our confessional separateness?

Communion with the crucified Son of God means for me that:

1. The church obtains its life and its unity *from* the cross of Christ.
2. Fellowship of Christians with one another will take place amid persecution and tribulation, that is, *under* the cross.
3. The redemptive suffering of God, the messianic suffering of the church, and the apocalpytic "suffering of these times" will end only when the joy of God in his redeemed, glorified, and united creation comes to fulfillment; the true church is the "people of the Beatitudes," who hope and suffer for its coming.

THE SOURCE OF THE CHURCH'S LIFE AND UNITY

It is certainly superficial to enquire about the church's "hour of birth," since dates tell us little about the wellspring of truth. If, however, one persists in asking about its origin, one is led from Pentecost and the outpouring of the Spirit upon all flesh to Easter and the vocation of the apostles. But Easter points unmistakably to Good Friday since it was as the Crucified One that Christ appeared to the disciples in the brilliance of the glory to come. They recognized him by his nail-inflicted wounds and by his breaking of the bread. The true origin of the church lies in the self-giving of Christ unto death upon the cross. The passion of Christ is vicarious suffering for the redemption of the world. Christ's death pangs are thus the birth pangs of the church, which extends his service of reconciliation to the people in this unredeemed world. From the suffering of the Messiah the messianic people is born, namely the people of the Beatitudes.

In the crucifixion of Christ, the divine mystery of his self-surrender is revealed, for this is the mystery of God himself. It is the mystery of the Trinity, open to the world, to time, and to humanity; the mystery of the compassionately searching love of God. The Father gives over the Son of his eternal love in order to become God and Father to the abandoned. In order to become Lord over the living and the dead, the Son is surrendered to this death and this hell. Through his surrender, the Spirit comes upon all flesh to make it eternally alive, to unite it with God, and, thus, to glorify it. Whatever else the church may grasp about her life and determine about her form, the fundamental mystery of the church is the mystery of the reconciling and redeeming death of Christ upon the cross. The deeper the various churches and Christian communities go in understanding this mystery of Christ's death, the better they understand the mystery of the church, its life, and its unity.

Where does the Crucified One meet us today? Surely not just in theological knowledge, conferences, or ecumenical meetings. He invites us to his meal where, at the Lord's Table, in a communion of eating and drinking, we experience his liberating fellowship with the many, and hence also with us. He who was sacrificed is present as the exalted and coming Lord to celebrate with us in eucharistic fellowship the feast of salvation, the "feast without end." It makes no sense to take great pains in excluding this point from ecumenical proceedings. If we are not merely speaking *about* the cross, but are rather speaking with each other *under* the cross, then the proper place for this is the Lord's Table in eucharistic fellowship. At any other meeting place we are not yet at the precise point where his presence is revealed to us. This is indeed the "sore-point" of all ecumenical efforts, but the Lord's Supper is also the "source-point" for communion between the Crucified One and ourselves, and for our communion with each other.

The separated churches are still like the disciples at Emmaus: They were near Christ since he came near to them and walked with them. They were by his side, yet they did not recognize him. They were walking on parallel paths and not coming together. In the same manner we Protestants celebrate the "Lord's Supper," the Orthodox their "Eucharist," and the Catholics their "Mass." Walking on our parallel paths, where are we going to come together? "When he sat down with them at table, he took the bread, gave thanks, and broke it and gave it to them. And their eyes were opened, and they recognized him" (Luke 24:30). How else then should we today recognize him and one another in his fellowship other than in this: that *he himself* breaks the bread for us and hands us the cup? That is to say, we recognize him at the meal of his communion, the communion of his body and his blood to which he himself invites us. His invitation, furthermore, is without limits and without conditions. The invitation to the eucharistic meal is the inviting request of the dying Christ who was handing himself over for us. It is the crucified Christ himself who invites the poor and the guilty to the table of God's kingdom. That is why his welcoming hands open as wide above the eucharistic meal as did his outstretched arms upon the cross. The invitation to eucharistic fellowship in his name is open to the world, excluding no one but including everyone. However, it is still a qualified openness. It is qualified by the bitter sufferings and death of the Son of man.

The more I see behind the mystery of the Lord's Supper the mystery of his self-surrender, the more clearly I hear in the invitation to the meal the invitation of the Crucified One. It is the appeal of the Christ in whom I live, who suffered and died for me and for the world. Therefore I see no reason why any church should hold back the open hands of Christ which are outstretched toward all. I find no right to refuse eucharistic fellowship to anyone who hears and responds to the invitation of the Crucified One. It is not the eucharistic fellowship of all Christians which must be justified; that is already justified by the right of Christ's grace upon the cross. Rather, what does need to be justified is every exclusion, every refusal, and every holding-back. But how can these be justified when we are dealing with the Lord's Supper and not with something arranged by a church? The Lord himself invites the poor to this meal in order to enrich them through his poverty; it is not just the invitation of a confessional body to its own members. The invitation to grant freedom and justification to the abandoned comes from the Friend of sinners and not from a particular group to its participants. Whoever takes the cross seriously begins to feel pain at the division of the churches. He or she takes part in the suffering of Christ who, through such divisions, is himself "divided" (1 Cor. 1:13). But this situation is intolerable and must be overcome.

THE FELLOWSHIP AMID PERSECUTION
AND TRIBULATION

Fellowship in spite of confessional barriers will be experienced and lived in practice when Christians collectively "take their cross" upon themselves. The living experience of "ecumenism at the grass roots" was and is today found in a common resistance to political idolatry and social inhumanity, a common suffering at the sight of oppression and persecution. The church of Christ, in its hour of truth, is the church under the cross. True discipleship becomes visible in such situations: "If any man would come after me, let him deny himself, and take up his cross and follow me" (Matt. 16:24). Thus, Christians and churches stand before a decision: "Whoever would save his life will lose it, and whoever loses his life for my sake will find it" (Matt. 16:25).

There are older persons among us who will remember how they or their friends experienced this kind of fellowship in Christ in the prison camps of World War II. Behind barbed wire fences traditional doctrinal differences of the divided churches no longer had any special relevance. Christians got together wherever they were, read the Bible, prayed together, and were strengthened in faith. In situations of need, intercommunion and co-celebration were not so problematic as to prevent Christians from sharing in the breaking of the bread. They asked only about the One who is truly important, and they experienced the presence of Christ amid sufferings. This gave them inner strength and firm confidence. Whether one was a priest or a lay person, a student of theology or a laborer, here there was no special precedence or privilege. Here the only things that really counted were the genuineness of faith, the commitment of the person, and the fellowship of confessing Christians. Each one was challenged and had to stand without the support of his or her tradition or the protection of the particular customs of his or her confession. In such a manner each one was tested in the fire of tribulation. Others have endured harsher sufferings in prisons and concentration camps. Those who survived such experiences returned to tell of the extraordinary fellowship they then felt with the suffering Christ and with one another. Confessional divisions had become alien to them, and now seemed purely external. These fellow sufferers had for a short time experienced a fragment of the one church of Christ, in the fellowship of Protestant, Catholic, and Free-Church Christians.

There are younger persons among us who will realize that ecumenical fellowship is being experienced in the same way today in the prisons of Chile, Korea, and other places—and not least in "socialist" countries. From the depth of shared sufferings and shared prayer a new fellowship comes into existence. The early Christians were convinced that "the martyrs of today are the seed of tomorrow's church."* The same is true today. Paul Schneider, Father Delp, Dietrich Bonhoeffer, and Maximilian Kolbe, along with the many nameless persons who gave up their lives, do not belong simply to one confessional community but to the whole of Christianity throughout the world. Through their deaths they speak to all who live and believe so that they may be one and may be free.

Ecumenical summit conferences between bishops and church leaders may go on. Conferences of theologians may solve contested theological points. But true and lasting ecumenical *unity* will be lived on the basis of united endurance and shared suffering. Only in the actual fellowship of the sufferings of Christ is the power of his resurrection experienced (Phil. 3:10). Only by sharing in the "suffering of these times" which comes upon all human beings is the coming glory of the new creation made certain for us. "When the Lord restored the fortunes of Zion," (Ps. 126), that is, when the prisons of our time are opened, then we shall be like "those who dream." Then shall we perceive the one church and forget our divisions and hostilities. The World Council of Churches in Geneva, the Secretariat for Ecumenism in Rome, the Ecumenical Patriarchate, and the many ecumenical communities and working groups in the churches which are allowed to operate publicly should always remain aware of the fact that the one church of Jesus Christ is already experienced in a form hidden under the sufferings of prisoners and in the silence of those who are not allowed to speak. Thus the names of such people as these should always be voiced in prayers of intercession at the beginning of every ecumenical act of worship.

What do we gain from this experience for our theological understanding of the church's unity? I think that we gain the realization that effective unity begins from fellowship in poverty and suffering. Naturally, we can also assemble the positive features of each separated church and tradition and build a many-sided, colorful ecumenical tower—an open temple with many different apartments where one serves the others with one's best. But leading to such a "heavenly Jerusalem" is the "way of the cross." Fellowship in the negative always precedes fellowship in the positive, and without this ecumenism of the negative, there will be no positive ecumenism either. There are many kinds of bread, according to the persecuted South Korean Cardinal Kim. There is the good white bread of friendship, but there is also the black bread of suffering, of loneliness, and of poverty. This is the bread in which splinters of wood have been mixed. This black bread of suffering should be fraternally divided. This must come first. True ecumenical unity begins precisely where we mutually share our poverty, our sickness, our inhibiting obstacles, and our stagnations. The hunger in India is our hunger. The despair in Chile is our despair. The prayers in Korea are our prayers. Ecumenism always begins with a fraternal sharing of suffering under the cross. "A sorrow shared is a sorrow halved," as the proverb has it. This applies also to the church and its unity. Communally endured persecution gives courage. Shared poverty brings enrichment in fellowship. *Ecumene* first comes into being under the cross in the negative sense. Ecumenical fellowship in the positive sense follows by itself, since the positive that we possess then belongs to no one person alone but is rather that which we have received in common, not only for one another but actually with each other.

Not every suffering of or in the church is a partaking in the "suffering of Christ." There is also a suffering caused by one's own inhibition. Even within the church there is a sort of self-pity and grief for the wrong reasons. When the church's influence is on the wane, its people are withdrawing from it, and its external power is reduced, then the church's turmoil cannot yet be equated with the suffering of Christ. The church shares in Christ's sufferings only when it takes part in Christ's mission. Its Christian suffering is apostolic suffering. As is seen in the case of Paul, Christian suffering involves blows, imprisonments, dangers, and contempt—bodily suffering which the apostle experiences in this world (2 Cor. 4:8; 11:23ff.). Insofar as Christians participate in the messianic mission of Christ, they also partake in his messianic suffering. Insofar as Christians live from the self-offering of Christ for the many, and for this same reason offer their own lives, they partake in the priestly sufferings of Christ. Insofar as Christians struggle and endure under the lordship of Christ, they partake in his condition as servant. The compassion of the church for the people derives from the messianic passion of Christ which fills Christianity with the Spirit of the new creation.

There are sufferings which cause Christians—and whole churches—to feel uncertain and doubtful. But there is also that suffering which makes faith certain and which renews the churches. Apostolic suffering, the suffering from witnessing to the gospel, and messianic suffering, the suffering of love and *unselfish* suffering for the sake of God's justice in the world, strengthen the faith and renew the church. Sharing in God's suffering in the world leads to the resurrection. For under this cross it is not our life, nor the life of the existing churches, but the life of Jesus which is "revealed to all mortal flesh" (2 Cor. 4:10). True faith is concerned with this alone.

THE PEOPLE OF THE BEATITUDES

The theology of the cross is not a one-sided theology of suffering. The acceptance of suffering in one's personal life has nothing to do with masochistic self-destruction. The cross of Christ stands in the light of his resurrection, and his passion stands as the sign of joy which love brings. Hence, the compassion of Christians also takes place in the strength of sharing

Christ's joy, and it serves to glorify God in his coming kingdom. Just as one cannot speak of Good Friday without Easter,
so one must not speak of the suffering of God without also pro-
claiming the joy of God. The mystery of God's suffering is not
a sad or tragic mystery, but one which liberates and is blessed.

We said above that the mystery of the Trinity reveals itself
to us in the mystery of the cross. Now we return to this point.
Inasmuch as God opens himself in searching love to our human history and enters into it through the self-offering of his
Son, he actually experiences this history. God is not a cold,
silent, heavenly power. He is not immutable in the sense of being incapable of being hurt by human refusal of his love.
Neither is he perfect in the sense of being perfectly content
whether or not his searching love actually finds those whom he
seeks and loves. The story of the searching love of God is essentially the story of God's "thirst and desire" for his image on
earth and, thus, the story of his suffering.* In his beloved Son,
whom he hands over to sin and death to redeem those who
were their subjects, God makes a discovery which has a profound bearing upon the redemption of the world. He experiences within himself the weight of sin, the death of abandon-
ment, and the hell of rejection. Therefore, God is glorified by
human beings in no other way than by the glorification of the
slaughtered Lamb. The cross of the Son is the eternal
signature of the lordship and reign of the Father. With the
sign of the cross the church is blessed, and with the sign of the
cross it blesses the world.

Just as many Christians cross themselves in the name of the
Trinity, so also must we understand God theologically in the
light of the cross and the cross in the light of the Trinity. In
view of Christ's accursed death and descent into hell, we can,
therefore, speak with Kitamori of the "pain of God," which is,
from the very outset, searching love.† In the dark night of
Golgotha God experienced suffering, death, and hell. In this
way God experiences history.

That, however, is not the end, but rather the way. God experiences the history of sin and death in this way in order to
create the future of salvation and life. He goes out from
himself in order to gather his creation to himself. He becomes

vulnerable in order to cure, and he endures the death of the Son in order to liberate. Where his suffering brings fruit and his passion comes to its conclusion, we can speak of the joy of God. There is "more joy in heaven over one sinner who repents than over ninety-nine righteous persons who need no repentance" (Luke 15:7). And those who come to the great banquet in God's kingdom are called to "enter into the joy of your Lord" (Matt. 25:21). The history of the liberation of human beings, the history of their gathering to the banquet of the Lord, and the history of their unification in the Spirit are nothing less than the history of God's joy. His joy in history will be perfected in his eternal beatitude in the kingdom of glory. Thus, the church's temporal sharing in God's joy will also be perfected in the beatific vision, the endlessly shared joy in the unlimited fullness of divine life.

The suffering of God leads to the joy of God, and God's pain in the world is the way to God's happiness with the world. In this perspective the resurrection of Christ is not simply the confirmation of the crucified Savior, but beyond that, it is his transfiguration. Just as grace now dominates where sin used to reign (Rom. 5:10ff.), so God's joy gains the balance over his suffering, and his blessedness finally has predominance over his pain. The story of God's suffering in Christ leads to the story of God's joy in the Spirit. In the completion of God's joy his suffering is certainly not cancelled, set aside, and forgotten; rather, it remains as fruitful, saving, renewing suffering and the basis of eternal joy in his kingdom.

The redemptive suffering of God, the messianic suffering of his people, and the sufferings of these times which extend through the whole world belong together. God's suffering leads on to blessedness when the whole creation will be redeemed. The suffering of the church with Christ and for the world will continue until the dawn of glory. Only when the longing desire for freedom is fulfilled for the whole of enslaved creation will the suffering of the church be transformed into joy. No matter how heavily suffering and sacrifice may weigh upon us or how severe the predominant forces of injustice and death may be, there are encouraging signs of joy and even more joyful songs of liberation to be heard within and under the passion of God and the world. In the light of the dying Christ the sufferings and griefs of death are not without hope. The transformation of suffering has begun.

From the cross and under the cross the church will understand itself as the people of the Beatitudes. In poverty with Jesus they are happy, and in happiness with Jesus they become poor. In endurance with him they are comforted, and in this comforting they can go on enduring. In the gentleness of his self-offering they possess the earth, and in this certainty they will prepare the way for a friendly world. In his Spirit they will hunger for righteousness and will, therefore, be persecuted. Amid their hunger and their persecutions they will have their fill. Ecumenical unity under the cross derives finally from this joy over God's kingdom which comes from his passion. Ecumenical unity, therefore, is also willing to endure the passion.

7

Hope in the Struggle
of the People

SELF-RESEARCH

Before I speak to anyone else about "hope in the struggle of the people," I must speak to myself. I will do that openly because I believe that each of us must research himself or herself before he or she can speak of a hope which is the hope of the people itself and not one's own ideology. When I first reflected on this theme, I thought, "Hope is good; I would like to say something about it." The longer I reflected on it, however, the more I had to ask myself, "Am I a man of the people? Who am I? For whom can I speak?" I began to research the levels of my own personality and to take a look into my own biography.

I am at the present time a professor at a state university in Germany. I am what they call "educated," an "academic." That distinguishes me from the "uneducated" nonacademicians, that is, from the people. I am, therefore, in the same situation as the Pharisees and the scribes in the time of Jesus, even if I have no intention of scorning the people, in New Testament Greek the *ochlos,* those masses of uneducated who have not studied and have not been able to keep the Torah. If I were merely such a "study man," then I could sit at my desk and think up beautiful educational schemes *for* the poor people and pronounce my hope *for* the people, but I would never speak *from* the people or *with* the people and could not say one word about the hope *of* the people.

In addition to being scholarly, academic theology is also pastoral theology. Our theological students also live in separation from the people who can no longer go to college or university. Our academic theology speaks with the Bible, the church fathers, and with other sciences and ideologies. But it does not speak the language of the people and does not express the experiences and hopes of the people. We research the theological concepts of earlier experiences but we seldom bring the contemporary religious experiences of the suffering or struggling people into new conceptuality. Our theological work thus separates us from the people. Therefore, the people do not understand us, and they view professors and students, even socialist academicians, with deep mistrust.

Furthermore, I come from West Germany, which is, as they say, a rich country. Those who must bear the cost of our wealth, immigrants admitted on work permits and workers in the Third World, do not feel understood or recognized by the German people, including the German workers; instead they feel degraded and oppressed. If I were to speak as a member of the German people, then people in other countries would not have the impression that I was speaking honestly about their suffering and their hope.

I was not always a professor of theology. For more than five years I was a pastor in a country farming community. In those years I experienced what a pastor of the *Volkskirche*, the "church for the people," can experience. I preached, taught, baptized, married, buried, and visited homes and the sick. As far as was possible I lived *in* the village, *with* the village, and *for* the village. In this situation there was no separation between university and congregation, but there was a difference between church people and their pastor, the people in their work clothes and the man in his robe. The pastor was supposed to be *for* them, but he could not be present *with* them, as one *of* them. He could preach hope to them but only they themselves could express their own hope and their own struggle. It helps me when as a professor of theology I can remember the experiences I had as a pastor in my congregation. It brings me a bit nearer to the people, but it does not yet bring me into the *Volk*, the people itself. Thus I must dig yet deeper into my biography.

In 1944 I was sent to the war at the age of seventeen. In 1945 I was placed in a prison camp with a mass of my people: three years of forced labor. We lost our names and became numbers. We lost our home and our country; we lost our hope and our self consciousness; and we lost our community. What we experienced in those years was *ochlos*, an unorganized, uneducated, imprisoned, and suffering mass of people without a face, without freedom, without history. It seems to me that as a POW I was in the people and nothing other than one of the people. When I saw the mud huts in the slums of Mathare Valley outside Nairobi I remembered the hovels in which we prisoners sought protection from the snow and rain behind the barbed wire. When I saw the insensible, expressionless faces and the stooped gait of the hungry people in the shantytowns, it all came back to me. I must also have looked like that: contorted, shabby, with hunger pangs in my stomach, despair in my heart, and a curse against God and humanity on my lips. I recognized myself in them. I believe in those years I was *Volk* and experienced what "the people" is.

These of course are old stories, and what young people are interested in the stories of their fathers? But for me these stories are important. Who am I? And as who do I reflect on the theme of "hope in the struggle of the people"? No one can slip out of his or her own skin, but everyone has more than one skin. I cannot help speaking as a professor of theology and as an academician. I cannot help speaking as a pastor. But I will try to speak also as a prisoner, as one of the people, and to use my experiences as a pastor and my possibilities as a professor to serve that community out of which I come and which has had a much deeper influence on me than anything that came later.

Russian dolls have inside them smaller dolls. One can take them apart until one comes to the core. Thus I will try to speak from the doll at the core inside my other wrappings and appearances, and I would like to ask you to try something similar yourselves—until each one of you has reached biographically that point where you are "the people" and nothing but the people, hungry and nothing but hungry, filthy and seeing only filth around yourself, struggling and thus having to hope, just as the people to whom the church or the Urban Industrial Mission has sent you.*

I am certain that many of you have more to say than I do and can say it more eloquently than I, because you can discover in yourselves more experiences of "the people" than I can. But without humbling ourselves in the lowliness of our own life I am convinced that we will not find the humiliated people even if we are in their midst and have contact with them every day. We will have in sight only our own actions and programs and consider ourselves benefactors of the people, but we will not really recognize the people themselves. We will end up trying sociology as a substitute because we do not find the history of the people's life and suffering in ourselves. We will commend *our* hope to the people but not experience the hope *of* the people. And the people will remain silent.

"THE PEOPLE"

"The people" is usually spoken of from the distance of the rulers. A king has his people whom he commands. When war comes, he issues a summons: "Forward, my people." But he himself does not belong to them. Further down in the order of rule one can notice that the classes and castes always speak of "the people" when they have in mind the others under them. They are the simple folk, the uneducated folk, the poor folk. Finally there are those who have no status, no power, no influence, who are so far under that they are not able to look down on anybody else. They are the unorganized, formless mass with which the others can do whatever they want. They are, as one says, the "plebians," the "vulgar mob," the "lumpenproletariat."

This downward distancing also happens in the language of the church. Before God, the Lord, everyone belongs in common to the one "people of God." The church is supposed to be "the people of God." But the pope, bishops, priests, and pastors then speak of the "church people" and mean the nonordained "laity," for whom they are supposed to officiate but who themselves have nothing to say. The expression "lay" originally meant a participant in what the New Testament calls *laos*, the people of God. As such, it of course included the pastor, priest, bishop, and pope. But today this term refers to an uneducated, nonordained, unconsecrated Christian who is taken care of by the officials of the church.

Theologians are professionals of Christianity; laity are not. In the words of J.B. Metz, this is the "church *for* the people," not the "church *of* the people."* Therefore the hierarchs are always trying to do the popular thing. They are affable, condescending, and solicitous so that the people will not be aware of their immaturity and their lack of control over their own future. The church wants of course to do something *for* the people. But precisely in doing this it proves that it does not belong *to* the people.

The language of rule does not contain within it the hope of the people in its struggles. The same is unfortunately true— almost without exception—with the language of the clerical church. In the eyes of the people the rulers and the ruling classes do not belong to the people. One regards them with fear and mistrust. One tries only to get along with them and not to attract attention. "Don't go to your prince unless you are called," said the German subjects, wanting to remain invisible. Or the people simply remain silent. "The silence of the people is the judgment of tyrants," runs an old European saying. Dictators therefore attempt to force agreement, approval, and one hundred percent elections, for the people's silence makes their dictatorial rule uncertain and deprives it of its legitimation. When silence becomes a way of life for the people, as is the case in South America, it becomes dangerous.

The people view the "church *for* the people" as a kind of religious supermarket in which divine wares are on sale. One pays unhesitatingly, when one can, for the ceremonies which have been ordered, but one has nothing to do with the business itself. People are constantly asking what a baptism, a wedding, or a mass might cost. People do not feel like responsible subjects in this church, whose only goal is to take care of them. In the "church *for* the people" the people appear only as objects.

"The people," however, is defined not only in the dimension of rule. There is also a collective identity which is characterized by a common language, history, and milieu. One experiences communion with a people because one speaks the same language and is Japanese, Korean, Indian, or Chinese. With the common language are combined common mores and customs and often also the memory of a common history. One becomes conscious of this collective identity especially when one encounters and lives with other peoples. Even in the common misery of the slums these collective identities work themselves out in different ways. Precisely here they are often excessively emphasized in order to elevate oneself over the others who do not speak one's own language and who have different customs.

In the language of the New Testament the people in this sense is not *ochlos*, but *ethne*. Even if peoples of different languages are suffering the same lot in the large cities, only seldom does there emerge in the slums a "melting pot" which draws them together. The consciousness of a common exigency, the necessity of a common struggle, and a hope which binds one to the other is strongly veiled by the identity of language, of race, and of clan. Even "the peoples" (*ethne*) will not gladly become "the people" (*ochlos*). Better a pogrom against the blacks and the Indians than to have to live with them on an equal footing.

For many it is just this ethnic and racial identity that is the only thing left to them in their misery and the only thing that proffers them an inner stability. The awareness that the common misery can be overcome only through common struggle and thus through community is generated quite slowly. The "international solidarity of the working class" is much stronger in speeches and programs than it is in reality. Under pressure from the German trade unions the immigrant workers are the first to be laid off in the new German unemployment. The situation is certainly not different in other countries. In an emergency everyone is his or her own neighbor.

There can be, however, no hope for humanity without a new understanding of *the people*, that collective entity made up of the various nations, languages, and races. Nationalism is one of the worst seductions of the people. It is an instrument of the domination of the people with which one people can be incited against another people. It is evil to "divide and conquer," to play with human anxiety about starvation and with the aggression to which it gives rise.

The collective identity of the people can also be determined by religion. Religion gives one the feeling of communion beyond the borders of nations and the limtis of language. Buddhists feel at home with Buddhists, Moslems with Moslems, and Christians with Christians even if they do not speak the same language. Like the communities of language, race, and culture, the religious communities are also ambiguous. They give the campesinos in their misery identity and community and the power to survive. They prevent people in the slums from becoming demoralized. Religion here is not an opiate of the people but a power of resistance not to be overcome by misery. The unemployed person is at least a Buddhist, a Moslem, or a Christian—and thus not a "nobody"! People who lose their religion and religious community often lose the rest of their will to live; they just give up.

On the other hand, the various religious identities in the common misery often lead to outbreaks of hate against others and to religous persecutions. Community beyond their boundaries can arise only out of an awareness of a common life space and of unification in a common struggle. There is hope only in a new collective identity of the people which takes up into itself also the ethnic and religious identities. Only then can the people protect itself in common against the threat that the various religious communities in its midst will be incited against each other.

I have maintained that "the people" is basically a concept of rule which signifies the ruled. But others also speak of "the people," namely, those who want to overthrow the old rule and establish their own system of rule. "The people" is mobilized to overthrow the old colonial rule and to set up a national caste rule. Paradise is promised to "the people" in order to realize an ideology.

Please pardon me if I am skeptical at this point. In Europe no one has sworn by the messianism of the people with more beautiful words than the fascism which in Germany we called "National Socialism." Hitler and Mussolini allegedly came from the people, presented themselves as "sons of the people," and passed for "liberators of the people." They promised to change a society divided by classes and castes into a new "commonality of the people." Through great national programs they eliminated unemployment: "one Volk, one Reich, one Führer." With this "folk"-ideology they subjugated the people to their rule and drove them into the war. In the end even children and the old and senile became part of the "people's company" [*Volkssturm*] for use on the front lines. Hitler committed suicide with the cynical words: "The German people is not worth me. May it be destroyed."

The people can also be exploited and destroyed with such ideologies for the "liberation of the people." The great seducers of the people always present themselves as the ostensible liberators of the people. One should be critical here and remain skeptical. What the people really needs, only the people can say. No rule and also no ideology is justified in doing that. Everything that allegedly is done or is to be achieved "for the people" is to be sampled with precaution. The people is not a means to an end, whether that end be bad or good. The people has its own worth. "Socialism *for* the people" turns out to be either doctrinaire or bureaucratic oppression of the people. True socialism is alone "socialism *of* the people."

JESUS AND THE PEOPLE

Christianity takes its bearings from the history of Jesus. It tells his story and it keeps on living his story. Communities are Christian insofar as in their storytelling they combine the story of their own sufferings and hopes with the story of Jesus. The New Testament story of Jesus is a collective biography which is open ahead. Thus, we should ask how "the people" appears in the story of Jesus, the disqualified *ochlos*, the mass without guidance and direction, the multitude without political and spiritual meaning, that group made up of men and women who have no firm community, no country, no home or family, who are unorganized and lack a collective identity.

It is precisely those persons who no longer have anything to lose who go to John the Baptist at the Jordan (Luke 3:7,10).

They come to Jesus to hear him, and in his presence to find
healing for their unhappiness. According to Matthew 9:36,
Jesus was "moved" by these people and "had compassion" for
them. In the original this means the pain went through his
heart. He could not get the existence and the situation of this
people out of his mind, nor could he restrain the people from
pressing around him. Their suffering came to him, went into
him, so that he had to—and wanted to—identify with them.
Jesus did not play down to them beneficently, but, as this text
says, he became one of them. He saw himself in this people.

The Pharisees and the scribes—the higher, organized
classes—are pictured as the opposite of this people. It is told of
them that they despised the people and cursed them as *massa
perditionis* (John 7:31,48ff.). Jesus and Paul were later accused of seducing the people (John 7:12; Acts 19:26). This
means that through Jesus and the apostles these people became
dangerous to the organized, higher classes in society. The people's wrath seldom breaks out, but it can become dangerous.
This is why Herod hesitated to execute the Baptist (Matt.
14:5). This is why the chief priests and the elders also hesitated
to arrest Jesus (Matt. 21:23-46) and above all sought to incite
the people against him. Finally in the visions of John there
emerges before the throne of God and the Lamb a people
(*ochlos*) of liberated ones which no one could number (Rev.
7:9). This multitude comes from all peoples, languages, and
nations.

Jesus identified himself with the people and he proclaimed
the gospel of the kingdom of God to these "poor" and made
present their liberation in words, parables, and healings. Did
Jesus become thereby the Savior *for* the people or the Messiah
of the people?

In order to search for an answer to this question we turn to
two well-known and oft-quoted stories.

In Matthew 25 we find the story of the "Great World Judge."
The Son of man, the Judge of the world, assembles humanity
before his throne, on his right and on his left. To those on his
right he says: "I was hungry and you gave me food . . . I was in
prison and you came to me." They are perplexed and answer:
"Lord when did we see you hungry and feed you or in prison

and come to you?" And the Judge answers: "As you did it to one of the least of these my brethren, you did it to me. Whoever visited them, visited me." But to those on his left he says, "As you did it not to one of the least of these you did it not to me." According to this story the coming World Judge is already present in the world, hidden in the hungry, the thirsty, the alien, the naked, the sick, and the imprisoned. And through Jesus this fact becomes open and revealed. One can know it. Because of the universality of the world judgment this cannot apply exclusively to the persecuted Christian brethren. Included here are all of the hungry. It is "the people." If this identification of the World Judge with the people is to be read anywhere, then it is in the passion of him who told this story: on the way of the hungry, thirsty, stripped, powerless Son of man from Nazareth to Golgotha.

What seems most important to me is the identification of the World Judge with the least of these, for it sounds strikingly similar to the identification of the exalted Christ with his missionary community: "As the Father has sent me, even so I send you . . . If you forgive the sins of any, they are forgiven; if you retain the sins of any, they are retained" (John 20:21,23). Thus are the apostles commissioned to the messianic mission of Jesus. They beseech, "On behalf of Christ, be reconciled to God" (2 Cor. 5:20). If here it is said, "Whoever hears you, hears me," so there it is said, "Whoever visits them, visits me."

In both cases it is a question of an identification by virtue of which Christ is present in and through others. In the case of the apostolate an identification with the active mission is prominent; in the case of "the least of these," an identification with the suffering expectation. In the apostolate the resurrected Christ speaks. Is it not the voice of the Crucified One which speaks from "the least of these"? If it is, then the church stands between the active mission of Christ ("Whoever hears you, hears me") and the passionate suffering expectation of Christ ("Whoever visits them, visits me"). How can the church of Christ live in the presence of the Crucified One in the poor, sick, and imprisoned people?

One usually reads Matthew 25 as a reference for Christian ethics, as the works of charity: one should feed the hungry, give water to the thirsty, give shelter to the stranger, and visit the imprisoned. But that is not enough. Matthew 25 does not make poor people into *objects* of Christian charity or of the Urban Industrial Mission, but *subjects* of the messianic kingdom, namely, brothers and sisters of Christ. Matthew 25 speaks of the hidden brotherhood of Christ—hidden in the brotherhood of the people—which must be part of the church's own self-understanding when it calls itself the brotherhood of Christ.

Where is the true church? The true church is where Christ is. Christ is present in the mission of the believers *and* the suffering of "the least of these." His community is therefore the brotherhood of the believers and the poor, the lovers and the imprisoned, the hopers and the sick. The apostolate says *what* the church is; "the least of these" say *where* the church belongs. Only if the church realizes in itself this double brotherhood of Christ does it really live in the presence of the crucified and exalted Christ.*

The Christ of the church was most often the exalted, heavenly King. But the Christ of the people was always the poor, homeless Son of man. Only where both become one does the church enter into the truth of Christ. So long as we think one-sidedly in missionary terms we think "from above to what is below," and we want to bring the church to the people. We desire to liberate and educate the people and bring it to the point where it can exercise its own power. However deeply we involve ourselves, it still remains mission *for* the people, and in it the people remain an *object* for our efforts. Matthew 25 tells us that and how "the least of these" are already subjects *before* the missionaries and helpers come! They are the brothers and sisters of Christ, the brothers and sisters of the World Judge ("Whoever visits them, visits me").

Missionary endeavor, and in particular that of urban industrial missions, before engaging in all programs of action and aid *for* the people should first discover Christ *in* the people and therewith the true messianic dignity of the hungry, sick, and imprisoned. That will allow one to be sensitive to more than manifestations of solidarity.

The other story that I would like to call to mind is the story of the eating and drinking of Jesus. Jesus identified himself with the people by eating and drinking with them. Important for him was the table community, especially with those who were despised as "sinners and tax collectors" by the better classes of society. They said contemptuously of Jesus: "This man receives sinners and eats with them" (Luke 15:2). What should we make of that? Just as Jesus proclaimed the gospel of the coming kingdom to "the poor" (and that means: God is coming and you can liberate yourselves; cf. Isa. 52), so he also anticipated with them the eating and drinking in the kingdom.

According to Isaiah 25 the coming God will prepare a great banquet with good wine for all *peoples* on his mountain. This is to be the feast of peace, of joy over the annihilation of death, and of full freedom in the presence of God. Jesus anticipates this messianic feast of the peoples (*ethne*) and he does it precisely with "the people," the *ochlos,* the "sinners and tax collectors" who cannot display the slightest righteousness in their own lives. The poor, the weak, and the powerless, who come from the "hedges and fences," that is, those who today come from the slums and the bush are his friends and table companions. They are the first with whom he celebrates the messianic feast and eats and drinks in the kingdom. These "last" have become "the first."

But Jesus also celebrated this eating and drinking in the kingdom of God with his disciples, obviously with a particular significance, "in the night in which he was betrayed." After that he did not want to drink any more wine "until the kingdom of God has come" (Mark 14:25). Thus this last supper was also meant messianically. The peculiarity of the table communion of the disciples with Jesus lies in the fact that in it they not only come into personal communion with him but they also participate in his messianic mission. With the disciples his mission not only reaches its goal, as with "sinners and tax collectors," but they are commissioned with his mission. It is not an exclusive meal of the pious, but the meal of the friends of Christ who take part in his mission to the poor "to seek what is lost." Therefore the friends of Christ will prepare the messianic feast for the people and eat and drink with them just as all will eat and drink in common in the kingdom of God. And where there is nothing to eat and drink they will provide what is necessary as they are able.

Mission does not mean only proclamation, teaching, and healing, but it also involves eating and drinking. Mission happens through community in eating and drinking. Hope is eaten and drunk. This is the eating and drinking mission of the kingdom. An old Jewish saying maintained, "The Messiah will come only when *all* of the guests have taken their places at the table." It assumes the overcoming of hunger in the world before the coming of the messianic time. The New Testament says that the Messiah Jesus has come so that *all* guests may sit at the table of the kingdom. It anticipates the overcoming of the peoples' hunger in the eating and drinking of the poor people. The eating and drinking mission anticipates the kingdom among the hungry and thirsty. That is its joy in its poverty.

Do these stories make Jesus a new religious lord of the people? No. He did not come to the people as their political and religious master to put them in their place, subjugated and quietly resigned. He did not force his own rule upon the people. Neither did he force his own form upon a formless mass. He heard the call of the people and called them out from their position as objects of the manipulation and rule by others to be subjects of the new history of God with the human race. The "folk movement" which Jesus enkindled is the movement in which the people itself becomes the subject of its own new history in the liberation movement of God.

Do these stories make Jesus a folk hero or a liberator of the people? Again I would say no. He did not mobilize the people for his own purposes. He always pointed away from himself: "Your faith has helped you." "The people" becomes the people of the coming kingdom and the coming kingdom becomes present through Jesus and his community. In Jesus the people discover their own identity and worth of which no ruler can rob them. But neither can this identity be relinquished to a liberator.

THE PEOPLE AS SUBJECT OF
ITS OWN HISTORY

Large, established churches have a difficult time with the people. Many of these churches understand themselves as hierarchy, that is, as "holy rule." Their officials, with every good intention to be sure, want to be true "shepherds" of the people. They seldom notice that using this image denigrates the people to a "flock of *sheep*" which one tends because one needs them. Other churches understand themselves as a community of believers who want to believe, confess, and live alike. They seldom notice that this community is also determined by the similarity of race, class, standards of life, and caste, and thus, certainly not with an evil intention, excludes others, namely, the people.

"The people" does not identify with either of these two forms of church. A silent disaffection with and loss of membership from these churches is spreading. The people is simply indifferent to these churches. Both churches are giving indications today that they have nothing to say to the people. Therefore they are making extraordinary efforts to become "church for the people," "church for the world," and "church for others," as the slogans say. They initiate action programs for "mission to the people" and allocate large sums for diakonic work which is supposed to help the people.

But does "the people" itself have something to say in these churches and their programs? Is there a way that the church *of* the people can develop out of the church *for* the people? How can the people become a subject in their church? When will the people take "the church," that is, the community with Christ, into its own hands? What is at stake in this question is the life of the church which takes its stand on Jesus. For the church of Jesus, as Metz has said, can more easily survive persecution by the powers that be and by its intelligent despisers than it can survive the doubt of the little people and the silence of the people.*

Urban Industrial Mission, if I understand correctly, began as a mission program of the church in the midst of the proletariat of the large cities. In this way it expressed the church's commission to mission and the solidarity of the church with the people. But with what intention?

The amazing Abbé Henri Godin, after living ten years as a worker priest in Paris, wrote a memorandum to Cardinal Suhard entitled, "Memorandum on the Conquest of the Proletariat for Christianity."* In my memory as a "prisoner with the people" I find this title offensive. The people are supposed to be reconquered for the church. What Christianity is, is obviously already defined by the church and the tradition. The people are supposed to agree to that which never really had anything to say to us and in which we also had nothing to say. Worker or prison priests who view themselves as *conquistadores* of the workers and prisoners on behalf of church and Christianity oppress the people in ways similar to the political *conquistadores*.

Others have inverted the intention of mission. Instead of seeking to bring the people into the church, they now want to bring the church into the people. That sounds better, but there is still the question, Which church? If the church is to be brought into the people, then it has obviously already been determined what the church is. It is what it was before it was brought into the people. What can the people do with it?

Recently mission has been conceived no longer in spatial but in historical and social terms. The mission of the church is the mission of God, and the mission of God is aimed at the total liberation of the whole enslaved creation to the kingdom of God and of freedom. "Within the perspective of UIM, the renewed church is one engaged in mission, participating in the action of God for the liberation of man."† This intention is good because it goes beyond the church to the liberating power of God. But it is still too closely tied to the old concept of the church *for* the people if it wants to liberate the people in the name of God and the power of his Spirit. The people remain mistrustful because they have already been so often liberated without becoming free. The programs of the missionary liberation of the people speak too little of the people themselves. The people themselves speak too little in them. For this approach to mission, community with other liberating people is sought. "Similarly, the church via UIM programs will be the ally of militant secular and political groups who affirm the same goal of liberation."* In praxis this alliance goes without saying. It is only to be questioned whether the liberators of the people are the liberated people themselves.

Urban Industrial Mission understands itself in view of the church as *mission*. It understand itself in view of the people and other political groups as *participation*. Neither of these is false, but it is not enough.

Mission is taking part in the messianic sending of Jesus and as such taking part in the people, with which he so much identified himself, to the extent that mission stands as a representative for him: "Whoever visits them, visits *me*." Therefore this mission should neither bring the people again into the church nor the church into the people, but rather discover the church *of* the people and live the brotherhood of Jesus in the brotherhood of "the least of these."

This happens best in and through basic communities and groups which live intensively with the gospel and their neighbors and which come together in prayer and in the breaking of bread. This can lead to a break with the churches as we know them up to now. But it cannot lead to a break with Jesus. The church *of* the people will then ask how it can become independent of the money, the programs, and the staffs of the missions of other churches. The talk of a "moratorium on Western missions" for the purpose of allowing the indigenous churches to become independent has, despite all misunderstandings, a kernel of truth: The indigenous, national churches should become the subject of their own history and therefore should become independent from other churches. The "world mission" should begin.

But can the brotherhood of Jesus in the people be realized and can the people become the subject of its own history with Jesus without a corresponding moratorium on Urban Industrial Mission? Or in what other ways can the people become free from the mission of the rich, the educated, the activists, and the ideologists in order to experience its own freedom in the kingdom of God? I have no answers, but I must pose the questions.

As POWs we were also cared for and tended to by the

YMCA and the British churches. An excellent staff worked for us outside the camp. We were thankful for all this. But if with our empty hearts and open hands we had not found the brotherhood of Jesus behind the barbed wire and experienced in it our own dignity, our own freedom, and our own hope, then I scarcely would have become a Christian and we would not have survived that time with our humanity. The community of the poor is of more worth than help and care from outside.

Participation is an expression of solidarity. When people have common goals, they work together. It is good to be engaged in this way. But in this common work people also criticize and correct each other. When we work in common with non-Christians for liberation, for human rights, and for the life of the people, *the people* must stand at the center in all of our commonality and in all of our mutual criticism—not as objects of our common efforts but as subjects of our common life. The functionary ideology and the staff mentality hinders this, for they separate an elite from the people.

It seems to me that the Christian community is singular in that it discovers Jesus in the people, and the people as the people of the kingdom. Before this community initiates programs and concludes historical alliances with other groups, it eats and drinks with the people and breaks the bread of poverty in the common hope. And when the persons of this community sit together in a circle and eat a common meal they can express their concrete needs and discuss the possibilities of common action and the strategies of self-liberation. Collective identity is practiced before it is promoted and mobilized. Participation means in the first place to eat, to drink, to live in common. It begins "in the belly," not in the head. One must savor it before one can speak about it. "First comes eating and then comes morality."* One can learn this from the history of the Messiah who eats and drinks with the people. Many times as POWs we received good supplies from outside. But our community really emerged only when we shared our bread rations even though no one's hunger was satisfied by it. But there was no longer any mutual stealing of breadcrusts. And when we were led out to the construction site we found community not with the sympathetic rich, but with the poor Scottish coal miners who also had nothing but who shared with us what they had. It sounds paradoxical, but shared poverty makes one rich. Divided wealth does not make one rich.

In conclusion my thesis is this: Hope in the struggle of the people is to be found in the people's becoming subjects of their own history. To take part in the community of Jesus means to take part in the history of the people and to rejoice with the people.

8

The Congregation "From Below"

REFORMATION OF THE CHURCH

Many people in our society, whether they be inside or outside or—as they like to say—"on the periphery" of the church, experience it daily as "church without community." One of these persons wrote: "When my wife and I moved to Stuttgart three years ago we were faced with the need to make contact with a congregation. We hoped for new human relationships. In the church we heard good sermons on which the pastor had spent much time and energy and which gave us a lot to think about. But our hopes for new genuine relationships with our fellow Christians with whom we sat in the pew were not fulfilled. We entered the church as isolated individuals, and we left it the same way."

Many persons who move to a different address in one of our cities find themselves involuntarily located in the territory of another neighborhood church. When they look into the church situation they are suddenly amazed to discover that they no longer "belong" to St. Matthew's Church but to St. John's Church and that it is no longer the former pastor but now a new one who is "at the disposal" of them and their children. No one has asked them and they could not decide for themselves. The question of church membership is still not a question of Christian free will. For this reason many come to church as separated individuals. For this reason many leave the church as separated individuals. For this reason many remain alone and at a distance. This church is not "their own thing" because their relationship to it is not a matter of their own decision.

But can *the* church be created through a preaching church which addresses each individual, and indeed, each individual in his or her own private world? Can it be done through a pastoral care church which takes care of each individual religiously, and indeed, each individual in terms of his or her private needs? Can it be done through a large national or cultural church with a rich catalogue of special offers for the people but without the people themselves? Where people experience the church as an institution in which they receive something but find no community, can such a church persist?

The Reformation promised something else. The promise of the Reformation was and is the congregation "come of age." The article with which the church stands and falls is, according to Luther, the doctrine of the justification of the sinner "for the sake of Christ," "without our earning anything, through faith alone." On this one basic assumption, according to Luther, Calvin, and many other Reformers of the sixteenth century, stands "everything we teach against the pope, the devil, and the world."* But this justifying faith is directly tied up with the calling of each and every Christian to life in the congregation. "Everyone who emerges from baptism is consecrated as priest and pope," said Luther. Thus the internal logic of this justifying faith gives rise to the "universal priesthood of all believers."

But where and how can this "universal priesthood of all believers" be realized and take on a form which is externally visible and credible? Certainly not in a hierarchical church of offices in which priests and laity are sacramentally distinguished from each other. And certainly also not in a state, national, or cultural church in which the political powers that be rule the conscience, or in which the conscience is accommodated to political pressures and economic interests. It can be lived credibly only in the gathered, mature congregation. It follows that the justifying faith with which the church stands or falls needs the independent congregation as its lifeform, and indeed calls it into being. Only this community which looks upon each person as a being with his or her own integrity and peculiar interests fulfills the Reformation commission which our fathers and mothers perceived in the gospel.

"The church" with its structures, organizations, and powers exists exclusively for the sake of the *congregation*. There is in the church nothing higher than the congregation. All ministries of the church are related to the congregation and are put to the test by the mature congregation. From its side, the congregation is mature to the degree that it no longer experiences itself as being taken care of ecclesiastically and tended to by ordained officials but rather becomes the independent, responsible subject of its own history with God. Only then can Christian freedom be experienced in the congregation, for only then will the congregation be experienced as the free zone of the Spirit of God.

In the hierarchical church with its splendid buildings and its wise authorities religious power was and is experienced as a reflection of the fatherly sovereignty of God in heaven. But God as love can be experienced and represented only in the comprehendible congregation in which one sees and recognizes the other, and accepts the other as he or she is accepted in Christ.

The gospel of the Christ crucified "for us" puts an end to religion as power and opens up the congregation's experience of God, the experience of love. Justifying faith thus puts an end to religious belonging and creates freedom in community.

This task of the Reformation can be expressed very simply: It is possible for a "parish to become a congregation."* It is possible for a church district to be replaced by a congregation which lives from its base in the people. It is possible that out of a church *for* the people which takes care of the people, there could come a church *of* the people, a *congregational* church. This is possible whenever and wherever the energies of the Spirit in the congregation are set free and no longer dampened. But is that worth wishing for? Is that offered in the gospel?

With this question we go first to the Reformation and to a Reformation concept which still has much to offer today.

THE FUTURE OF THE REFORMATION

Does the Reformation still have a future? This sounds like a curious question. It is curious because Reformation celebrations are usually concerned only with the past of the sixteenth century and the present of the twentieth century. In the nineteenth century on the anniversary date of Martin Luther's famous posting of the Ninety-five Theses everyone proudly glanced backward at the radiant past of this German man of God. Everyone praised the victory over the dark, papal Middle Ages and celebrated the freedom of faith, conscience, and religion which appeared in the modern Protestant world. Since the breakup of the Protestant-bourgeois world in world wars, revolutions, and inflations the backward glance is often made in anger today. In place of the Protestant self-consciousness appears a peculiar Protestant self-hate. It is no longer interested in the success but in what Wolfhart Pannenberg has called the "failure of the Reformation."* And this failure of the Reformation is measured by the standard of the church's unity. Responsibility for the "separation of the Protestant special churches from the one, Catholic church," the consequent "church division," the religious wars, and the emergence of the secular world is then laid at the doorstep of the Reformation. Consequently one seeks the "fulfillment of the Reformation" in the "restoration of the unity of the church" today. It is to be achieved through the recognition of the Reformation doctrine of justification by the teaching office of the Catholic church and, on the other hand, through the recognition of the papal primacy (as the unity-establishing office in the church) by the Protestant churches.

Now the unity of the church is certainly important. It may not be petulantly toyed with. In a humanity which is today being destroyed through its divisions and enmities, the unity of Christianity would be a sign of hope for survival which should not be underestimated. But the church does not arise out of a human vision of unity. Unity does not bring salvation, but salvation creates unity. The unity of the universal church can be organized through synods and offices of leadership only when unity already exists at the grass roots level. This unity, however, does not signify "the highest office in the church," but rather the existing "community." The Reformation consequently can be "fulfilled" only if its own impetus comes to the fore, not however if it is broken off. The Reformation's own impetus was and is composed of three strands: the justifying faith, the universal priesthood of all believers, and the mature, responsible congregation.

Whenever people look backward at the Reformation, whether with pleasure or anger, they often speak only in general ecumenical terms about "Evangelical and Catholic," "Protestantism and Catholicism." But it seems to me that the "future of the Reformation" does not lie on the right wing with its Catholic tendencies but on the so-called left wing of the Reformation, namely, with those who through ever new attempts and under constant persecutions have sought to realize "the congregation." They were called "Schwärmer" and "baptists" and "sectarians," and they were rejected. But they sought in truth "the radical Reformation." After the "reformation of doctrine" through the gospel they wanted the "reformation of life" through love. After the "reformation of faith" they wanted the "gathering of the congregation." In the sixteenth and seventeenth centuries they were persecuted by the governments and the state churches. Today we see ever more clearly that they remained true to the claim of the Reformation: justification through faith grounds the right to congregation. Luther's treatise, "That a Christian Assembly or Congregation Has the Right and Power to Judge All Teaching and to Call, Appoint, and Dismiss Teachers" was the beginning point for the free-church movement in Protestantism. Whatever forms the free churches in England, America, and then, since the beginning of the nineteenth century, also in Germany have developed (and there are of course dangers, mistakes, and wrong developments enough here too), the future of the church of Christ lies in principle on this wing of the Reformation because the widely unknown and uninhabited land of "the congregation" is found here. The Catholic dioceses and the Protestant national churches and denominations are today on the threshold of discovering the congregation. And it is no accident that everywhere in the old territorial church structures today grass roots congregations are arising—Christian communities, cells, and groups which are changing the church from the inside out and making it into the congregation. There is a great hope in the church; it comes from below, from the grass roots. After Catholic theology has for years envisioned the congregation as the church of the future, Protestant theologians are remembering this hope of the Reformation and this experience of the church struggles in the 1930s and 1940s. The congregation as the future of the church will be ecumenical. Precisely for this reason it can be called the fulfillment of the Reformation.

THE CHARACTER OF THE COMMUNITY

The Apostles' Creed immediately refers to the church as "the communion of saints." The Reformers perceived that personally. As the declaration of faith for the church they understood that the church is the community of justified and sanctified sinners. A church without this community of human beings with one another is no church of Christ.

The Augsburg Confession in Article VII interpreted this understanding of the church more exactly: the church is "the assembly of all believers among whom the gospel is preached in its purity and the holy sacraments are administered according to the gospel."* The congregation here is concretely the gathering: no community exists without gathering at a specific place at an appointed time and for definite activities. What defines this gathering is the proclamation of the gospel according to the scriptures and the administration of the sacraments according to the gospel. It is these two factors which distinguish this gathering and this community from an association or a club or a party. The Reformers were so clever as to maintain at the end of this same Article that "the true unity of the Christian church" depends solely on the unity created by the proclamation of the gospel and the practice of the sacraments. Everything else—cermonies and organizations—may be freely discarded. This is quite understandable seen against those times.

Today we see that it is not enough to assume that these statements would be sufficient to guarantee a mature congregation. The shortcoming in the Augsburg Confession is not that even in our time we might have to have a certain kind of leadership to assure the unity of the church. Rather what is lacking is that the community which is defined by the Word and the Lord's Supper must also be a community of love in mutual compassion and sacrifice. Whether the Reformation confessions speak of the "communion of saints" or the "gathering of the believers" nothing is changed in the church reality to which they refer. The individuals in the church are defined here only in terms of their relationship to God but not in terms of their relationship to each other. The community in the Spirit and the form which love gives to life do not yet come to expression.

The Barmen Declaration of 1934 reminded us of this problem. In Thesis 3 it maintained: "The Christian church is the community of brothers."* The congregation of brothers lives in the community with Jesus whom Paul calls the "first-born among many brothers." It demonstrates this through its brotherly life together and through standing up for each other in a society which is otherwise often unbrotherly. Brotherliness here comprehends this total life, not only life in the church and not only the life of the clergy. Brotherliness means a further contrast to secular society: in the congregation of brothers and sisters the relationships of master and slave, of ruler and ruled are to cease. Privileges and dependencies come to an end: "It shall not be so among you" (Matt. 20:26). In the brotherly community ownership and property titles are abolished: "And all who believed were together and had all things in common" (Acts 2:44). The brotherly community of Christ demonstrates the kingdom of God and the freedom of the Spirit through one intentional alternative lifestyle of the community.

The understanding of the church as a "congregation of brothers" has only two deficiencies:

The first deficiency is that it leaves out sisters. As was already the case with the fathers of the French Revolution, the fathers of Barmen failed in understanding the need for sisterhood along with brotherhood. "Brotherhood" was supposed to comprehend everyone. But if the congregation takes seriously Galatians 3:28, then there is in Christ not only "neither slave nor free" but also "neither male nor female"—all are one in him. It is to be hoped that this defect can be eliminated.

The second deficiency has to do with the fact that no one is able to select his or her brothers and sisters. In the figurative sense one can only "drink to" brotherhood or "renounce" it. Siblinghood cannot be terminated. Even in a conflict a brother remains one's brother and a sister one's sister. In order to enforce the element of voluntariness over against the coercion of belonging in the church, we should begin with the friendship of Jesus in order to comprehend the congregation of brothers and sisters also as the community of friends.

Friendship happens among free human beings. Friendship combines affection for the other with concern for the freedom of the other. Friendship can therefore be called the concrete life of freedom. The "brothers and sisters" make love necessary. But friendship lets love be free. In friendship love becomes an uncoerced respect and an uncoercing affection. Should we not therefore experience and form the Christian congregation as the community of friends who in the friendship of Jesus live with one another and in their common life live for the "sinners and tax collectors," the forsaken, and the helpless?

What is the community like which characterizes the congregation of Christ? I believe that the way from the "communion of saints" through the "assembly of believers" and the "community of brothers (and sisters)" to "open friendship" is the way to experience the presence of Christ ever more deeply and more surely. Thus every reform of church orders and organizations should begin with the experience of community at the grass roots. How can "communion" and "gathering" and "brother/sisterhood" and "friendship" be realized in the church?

THE CHURCH *FOR* OR *OF* THE PEOPLE

The Protestant national and cultural churches which we still have in West Germany derive, so far as their Word and Spirit are concerned, from the Reformation, but in their actual form as state churches they continue to be products of the "Constantinian era." This is a contradiction which must be eliminated. The Roman emperor Constantine made out of persecuted Christianity an "accepted religion" *(religio licita)*, and his successors elevated Christianity to the "official state religion"*(religio publica)*. As a result, the entire Roman Empire stood open to the mission and spreading of Christianity. But the Christian church had to pay a high price for this. It had to take over the role of "political religion" which was necessary for the ideological integration of the peoples in the Roman Empire. In this way the church "reached" all human beings. But as what? It reached all human beings as a part of the overall political order, namely, as the religious system of the social system. This has been the internal contradiction of the church since the Constantinian era began.

With the christianization of the Roman Empire the church sacrificed its peculiar and visible form as the congregation. Thus the church was no longer formed through voluntary and independent congregations but through belonging to regions, zones, parochial territories, provincial churches, cultural churches, and national churches.

The church district was ordered according to the residential quarters of the population. Church events became a part of the public routine. The offices of priest and bishop gained the authoritarian character of the *Herr Pastor*. The separation of the clergy from the laity became final. Faith was practiced by participating in the public events of the church. In place of the sacraments such as baptism and the Lord's Supper, which were meant to be celebrated by the community, there appeared the official acts of the priests. In place of community *in* the church there appeared the various grades of community *with* the church. In all this the church gained a public influence hitherto unheard of. But it lost its shape as a congregation, and therewith also its Christian diakonia. Diakonia was dissolved into the state's general welfare system, and with this the church also lost its mission. Mission was dissolved as the coerced christianization of the oppressed peoples came to the fore.

Was the Christian form of the community totally lost in the

church? It would be one-sided if one were not to see that there was appearing concurrently with, and indeed because of the "Constantinian era," an immense blossoming of Christian communal orders. Here in these close, inclusive circles the community whose existence was no longer possible in the large churches was experienced in radical discipleship, in freedom from property, and in contemplation and work. Without the cloister communities and the lay brotherhoods and sisterhoods, the great churches probably would have been transformed without resistance into a political religion. They would have forgotten the cross of Christ and the kingdom of freedom. The coexistence of large churches and Christian communes, of world openness and radical discipleship marks the double form of Christian life since Constantine.

For the Reformers this duality of the Christian life was intolerable. They believed that through the justifying faith *every* Christian is called to the status of true Christian. In this faith the difference between the status of the laity and the status of the orders is eliminated. In place of the twofold life-form of Christianity in cloister and world the Reformers wanted to realize the principle of one congregation in the midst of the world. Monasticism and cloister life therefore vanished from the Protestant churches. Unfortunately, the Reformers who denied monasticism did not formulate a comparably clear denial of the state church. Quite to the contrary, from 1525 on Luther and Melanchthon hindered the building of independent community by supporting the Protestant congregations which fell under the supervision of the Electorates. Only in the confessionally mixed regions, as for example in Niederrhein, were the Protestant "congregations under the cross" able to realize the Reformation hope in the congregation.

Today we stand in a situation of transition—certainly not a dramatic, spectacular change but a slow and persisting transformation. From a statistical perspective, the quantity of the Christian life is decreasing, but in spite of that, the quality of Christian life is rising in many congregations. The number of people who attend Sunday morning worship services is decreasing, while the number of participants in voluntary groups of spiritual, diakonic, liturgical, and political tasks is increasing. To the degree that the church which takes care of people "from above" is becoming ineffective, there is emerging at the basis a process of becoming independent. Along with this process the "congregational church from below" is appearing.

Pastors, church leaders, and theologians should not hinder this development but press for it, and if they feel obligated by the Reformation they must themselves be engaged in it.

But we members of the congregation should no longer feel that the pastors and official leaders of the church have relieved us of our own commission. We have delegated too many tasks to specialists. Thus our own powers are becoming stunted. When we begin by looking to the clergy for relief from our commission we end in alienation. Every Christian is called to tell others of the gospel and for this every Christian, not just the learned theologian, has a capability. Every Christian, not only the trained counselors in the counseling center, is called to the spiritual care of others in his or her house and among his or her acquaintances. We must bring diakonia back into the congregation. Diakonia in special associations or organizations is necessary, but the rebuilding of congregational diakonia can relieve large organizations, and Christian diakonia can guard against slippage in state welfare systems. We also have to bring mission and the *ecumene* back into the congregation and may no longer feel relieved from ecumenical objectives by supracongregational structures. As long as we view the congregations as local units of the regional or denominational church, we will remain impotent and passive. Only when the congregations become organizationally and financially independent and out of their own power regard themselves as subjects, can the supracongregational structures do their work without alienating the congregations.

It is not too important where one begins in all of this. What is important is that everyone begins where he or she stands and with the powers which he or she has. Thus, I will make several open-ended proposals with this in mind:

1) Our worship services are still too clerically and pastorally organized. They are events *for* the congregation, not yet events *of* the congregation. This situation can change:

—when the Lord's Supper again becomes the center of the worship service,

—when time is made available for spontaneous expressions,

—when all people in the congregation mutually greet each other,

—when everyone can be together in genuine fellowship happenings,

—when not only the minister but also the congregation prays and speaks,

—when the process of transposition from hearing to speaking the gospel can take place already in the gathering of the congregation itself,

—when we more frequently arrange festive gatherings of the whole congregation.

In place of a religious ceremony *for* the people each Sunday there can be a feast *of* the congregation. Then perhaps we would no longer be counted each Sunday as a church "attender" or a "guest" at the Lord's Supper but could actually feel "at home" in the congregation.*

2) On the question of church membership we should no longer consider just "belonging" and "standing" but should increasingly pay attention to the freedom of decision and the voluntary nature of faith. The fundament of the established church *(Volkskirche)* was and is infant baptism. Through it, involuntary belonging was and is prescribed from generation to generation. Should we not find an intentional, though thoughtful, way of moving from the established church practice of infant baptism to the congregational practice of baptizing those who are called? When newborn children are presented to the congregation, they are blessed, and in and through the infants the people are called to Christian service on their behalf. This, however, does not constitute the sacrament of baptism. A person should come to baptism after baptismal instruction in order to combine his or her own yes with the gracefully approaching Yes of God. Whoever dares to baptize his or her children as children on the basis of their future

---

* [In Germany a participant in a worship service is actually called a "church visitor" *(Kirchenbesucher)* and a partaker in the Lord's Supper a "guest" *(Abendsmahlgast)*— Trans.]

faith may not be denigrated. But by the same token the person who does not want to take from his or her children the joy of conscious baptism grounded in calling and confession should no longer be considered an outsider. When one observes how in the big cities the number of infant baptisms is rapidly sinking, and conversely, how in the United States the so-called voluntary religion of the Baptist congregations is flourishing, then we may no longer tie the destiny of the church to the practice of infant baptism. We should not allow ourselves to get caught up in the trend of secularization but should learn to esteem with all appropriate speed the personal freedom for baptism. Membership in the church without free will can no longer be accepted, but membership on the basis of free will is still valid.

3) For this reason everything depends on the emergence of small, freely constituted, comprehendible communities in the large, uncomprehendible districts of the church. Community exists only when persons really know each other. God as love is experienced not in large organizations and institutions but in communities in which people can embrace each other. Whether or not we live in a "mass society," the social isolation of the individual has become a kind of mass sickness. This is why many seek an intimate and, to be sure, a voluntarily formed community—because only such a community allows freedom and offers a free space. We should therefore strengthen free associations at the base of the churches so that they may become the living cells of tomorrow's congregation. Church leaders do not need to overburden themselves with responsibility for everything. They could allow "a hundred flowers to bloom" and expand the "market of possibilities" in the congregations.

Let us make the congregation strong. The large supra-congregational organizations of the churches often relieve the congregations of independence and responsiblity. But in the last analysis, in the times of contempt and persecution, the church stands or falls with the gathered congregation and with no one else.

The individual who comes alone to church and returns home alone is powerless. He or she suffers from inner doubt and remains a pawn in the hands of first this and then that power. Only in the gathered congregation does the believer become ready for action and capable of resistance. Hope in the midst of the conflicts of our society is embodied not just in the individual Christian or the large church structures which exist to care for the people. Hope is embodied in the congregation which exists in the friendship of Christ and can accept each person in his or her own integrity. The congregation is the lively hope because it is the experienced hope, the hope which has the power to enliven us in the midst of death. Therefore, make the congregation strong!

Notes

Page
13.   *Friedrich Schleiermacher, *The Christian Faith*, trans. H. R. Mackintosh and J. S. Stewart (Philadelphia: Fortress Press, 1977), p. 3.
24.   *Bertolt Brecht, "Die Dreigroschenoper," in *Gesammelte Werke*, vol. 2 (Frankfurt: Suhrkamp, 1967), p. 497.
42.   *Dietrich Bonhoeffer, *Letters and Papers from Prison*, the enlarged edition, ed. Eberhard Bethge (New York: Macmillan, Co., 1972). †Dietrich Bonhoeffer, "Thy Kingdom Come," in John D. Godsey, *Preface to Bonhoeffer* (Philadelphia: Fortress Press, 1965), p. 28. Trans. altered.
44.   *Roger Schutz, *Festival* (London: SPCK, 1974), pp. 69 ff. Trans. altered.
50.   *Joan Walsh Anglund, *A Friend Is Someone Who Likes You* (New York: Harcourt, Brace & World, 1958). †Ernst Bloch, *Das Prinzip Hoffnung* (Frankfurt: Suhrkamp, 1959), p. 1628.
51.   *Immanuel Kant, "The Metaphysical Principles of Virtue," *The Metaphysics of Morals*, pt. 2, §46 f. (Indianapolis: Bobbs-Merrill Co., 1964), pp. 135 ff. †Brecht, *Gesammelte Werke*, 12:389.
52.   *G. F. W. Hegel, *The Philosophy of Right* (Oxford: Clarendon Press, 1952), p. 228.
54.   *G.F.W. Hegel, *Lectures on the Philosophy of Religion*, vol. 3 (New York: Humanities Press, 1974), pp. 89 ff.
58.   *Aristotle *Nicomachean Ethics* 8. 3-8.
59.   *Karl Barth, *Church Dogmatics*, III/3, trans. G.W. Bromiley and R.J. Ehrlich (Edinburgh: T. & T. Clark, 1961), pp. 285-88. †Ibid., pp. 285 ff.
62.   *Goethes Werke*, vol. 1 (Wiesbaden: Insel-Verlag, 1949-52), p. 74.
63.   *Friedrich Nietzsche, *Thus Spake Zarathustra*, pt. 1, §16, in *The Philosophy of Nietzsche* (New York: Random House, 1927), p. 64.
64.   *Friedrich Nietzsche, *The Will to Power* (New York: Random House, 1968), p. 484.
67.   *Mircea Eliade, *The Myth of the Eternal Return*, trans. W. R. Trask (New York: Pantheon Books, 1954).
68.   *F. J. J. Buytendijk, *Das Menschliche: Wege zuseinem Verständnis* (Stuttgart: K.F. Koehler, 1958).
69.   *Felix Timmermans, *Pallieter* (New York: Harper & Row, 1924). †Karl Marx, *Basic Writings on Politics and Philosophy*, ed. L. S. Feuer (Garden City, N.Y.: Anchor Books, 1959), p. 263.
72.   *Johann Christoph Friedrich Schiller, "Der Antritt des neuen Jahrhunderts," in *Schillers Werke*, vol. 1 (Stuttgart: Deutsche Verlags-Anstalt, 1877), p. 214. †See Schutz, *Festival*, pp. 130 f.

73. *Quoted by Hugo Rahner, *Man at Play* (New York: Seabury Press, 1972), p. 86.
†See F. Stephun, *Dostojewskij und Tolstoj* (Munich, 1961), p. 29.
‡Aquinas *Summa Theologica* 3. 60.3.
76. *Erich Fromm, *You Shall Be as Gods* (New York: Holt, Rinehart & Winston, 1966), p. 194.
†Ibid., p. 199.
77. *Herbert Braun, *Jesus* (Stuttgart: Kreuz Verlag, 1969), p. 84.
†Ernst Käsemann, *New Testament Questions of Today* (Philadelphia: Fortress Press, 1969), p. 191.
78. *Quoted by Josef Pieper, *In Tune with the World: A Theory of Festivity*, trans. Richard and Clara Winston (New York: Harcourt, Brace & World, 1965), p. 18. Trans. altered.
†See Gerhard M. Martin, *Fest: The Transformation of Everyday*, trans. M. Douglas Meeks (Philadelphia: Fortress Press, 1976).
80. *Sir Walter Scott et al., trans., *The Complete Works of Johann Wolfgang von Goethe*, vol. 5 (New York: P. F. Collier, n.d.), p. 189. Trans. altered.
†Pieper, *In Tune with the World*, pp. 17-24 and passim.
83. *Cf. David P. Gaines, *The World Council of Churches: A History of Its Background* (Peterborough, N.H. : Richard A. Smith, 1966), pp. 17-23.
†Oliver S. Tomkins, ed., *The Third World Conference on Faith and Order Held at Lund* (London: SCM Press, 1953), p. 15.
89. *Tertullian *Apology* 50. 13.
92. *Lady Julian of Norwich, *The Revelations of Divine Love*, trans. James Walsh (New York: Harper & Brothers, 1961), esp. chap. 75, pp. 191-93.
†Kazoh Kitamori, *Theology of the Pain of God* (Richmond: John Knox Press, 1965).
97. *Chapter 7 of this book was originally presented as a lecture to the Urban Industrial Mission Conference, Tokyo, March 1975.
99. *Johannes B. Metz, "Kirche und Volk oder der Preis der Orthodoxie," *Stimmen der Zeit* 192 (1974): 797-811.
105. *Benoit Dumas, *Los dos restros alienaolos de la Iglesia una* (Buenos Aires, 1971).
108. *Metz, "Kirche und Volk."
109. *Cf. Émile Poulat, *Naissance des Prêtres-Ouvriers* (Tournai-Paris: Casterman, 1965), esp. pp. 36-51. The memorandum was later expanded and included in different form in Henri Godin, *France: A Missionary Land?*, trans, and ed. Maisie Ward (London: Sheed & Ward, 1949).
†"Struggle to Be Human," a pamphlet published by the Urban Industrial Mission, 1974.
110. *Ibid.
111. *Brecht, "Dreigroschenoper," p. 457.
114. *"The Smalcald Articles," *The Book of Concord*, trans. and ed. Theodore G. Tappert (Philadelphia: Fortress Press, 1959), p. 292.
115. *H. M. Schulz, *Damit Kirche lebt. Eine Pfarrei wird zur Gemeinde* (Mainz: Matthias Grünewald, 1975).
116. *Wolfhart Pannenberg, "Lebensraum der christlichen Freiheit. Die Einheit der Kirche ist die Vollendung der Reformation," *Evangelische Kommentare* 8 (1975), pp. 387 ff.
118. *Book of Concord*, p. 32.
119. *John H. Leith, ed., *Creeds of the Churches* (Richmond: John Knox Press, 1973), p. 520.